THE GREAT WINE PYRAMID

John & Shari Rudy

Cheers!
John & Shari Rudy

BRUNDAGE PUBLISHING

THE GREAT WINE PYRAMID
by

John & Shari Rudy

BRUNDAGE PUBLISHING
Room 203 Executive Office Building
33 West State Street
Binghamton, NY 13901

www.BrundagePublishing.com

Feature and recipe contributions by J.C. Rudy
Front cover by Ruben Acevedo
Feature graphics by Betty Tuininga
Wine Wit cartoons by Bob Johnson

Edited by Nicole L. Kradjian

Library of Congress Control Number: 2006929213
ISBN Number: 1-892452-48-4

Printed in the United States of America

THIS BOOK IS DEDICATED TO YOU

CHEERS!

TABLE OF CONTENTS

DESSERTS   187

MISCELLANEOUS

INTRODUCTION

W hen in doubt, add more wine!

Cooking with wine has always inspired delicious entrées, but *bella vino* doesn't have to entice your taste buds only for special occasions. (Besides, cooking with wine makes it a special occasion!) Wine can be used in your everyday cooking process as a marinade, to de-glaze a sauté pan or to finish a dish. In this book, we share more than 140 recipes for wine-enhanced dishes, many of which were contributed by wineries from all across the country.

As a former mathematics instructor, I used to share with my students that $1 + 1 = 2$, however I've found cooking with wine to be an exception. When the right wine is added to the right dish, the combined ingredients become more than the sum of the individual parts . . . and something magical happens.

As you embark on this taste adventure, you will discover simple ways to transform ordinary dishes into extraordinary dishes. The key lies in the use of wine as a taste blender and flavor enhancer.

We've grouped the recipes in this book into categories identified by the USDA Food Pyramid: Grains, Meats and Beans, Vegetables, Fruits and Milk . . . as well as that unofficial but delicious category: Desserts. Like salt and pepper, wine has tremendous value in everyday cooking, and it can be used quickly and easily in a wide variety of dishes.

So pull out the apron, grab a glass of wine and let's get cooking! Good food and good wine. . . now there's a perfect pairing.

                                                  John

For additional information, visit **thewinepyramid.com**

USING THIS BOOK

R ecipes:

In this book, you will find more than 140 fabulous wine recipes to drive your taste buds wild. Recipes are divided into six food groupings on the wine pyramid. There were additional recipes to share and so we added a seventh food grouping that we are calling the Miscellaneous Group. For each of these food groupings, there are more than ten delicious recipes.

Each recipe throughout the book has a difficulty rating assigned to it. This rating will give you some guidance concerning the difficulty and time required to prepare the recipe. On a scale of one to five wine glasses (♀) one wine glass means the recipe is extremely easy to make and five wine glasses means it requires more culinary expertise. **Please note that, unless otherwise indicated, preparation times given in this book include baking times.** The authors have selected their favorite recipe in each section. You will find a star (*) next to the recipe name in the Table of Contents.

S pecial Features:

Buzz on the Vine: Read high-interest features on topics such as "how to flambé", "hosting a wine party" and "celebrity wineries".

Cellar Challenge: Do you know all there is to know about wine? Test your prowess with the fun quizzes throughout this book.

Corkboard: Enhance your wine IQ with interesting facts and trivia. Learn some of the reasons why this beverage is so intriguing to so many.

Wine Wisdom: Many have made memorable comments about wine over the centuries. In this feature, you will read some entertaining quotes.

Wine Wit: Enjoy humorous cartoons by the hilarious Bob Johnson.

Wine Words: This feature includes tasting and winemaking terms to help you sound like a professional.

ACKNOWLEDGEMENTS

What a delight it has been to get to know the chefs, winemakers and other wine aficionados who have contributed approximately half of the recipes contained in this book. It is with our most heartfelt thanks that we acknowledge:

Andretti Winery * Artesa Vineyards and Winery * Baldwin Vineyards * Bargetto Winery * Baywood Cellars * California Wine Club * Callaway Vineyard and Winery * Fall Creek Vineyards * Firestone Vineyard * Gnekow Family Winery * Hinzerling Winery * Husch Vineyards * Jordan Vineyard and Winery * Kenwood Vineyards * Korbel Champagne Cellars * Lake Sonoma Winery * Lambert Bridge Winery * Los Pinos Ranch Vineyards * Martin & Weyrich Winery * Mill Creek Vineyards and Winery * Mission Hill Family Estate * Mount Palomar Winery * Oakstone Winery * Pedroncelli Winery and Vineyards * Peju Province Winery * Perry Creek Winery * Pleasant Hill Winery * Preston Premium Wines * Retzlaff Estate Winery * Sebastiani Vineyards and Winery * Stevenot Winery * Thornton Winery * Valley of the Moon Winery * Van Ruiten Vineyards * Ventana Vineyards and Winery * wineloverspage.com *

To find out more about them, or to order their extraordinary wines, please visit their websites. Many offer other great recipes as well.

WINE BASICS

Wine is a wondrous pleasure to enjoy. Fortunately, one can enjoy it without needing to be a wine expert. If you are new to the world of wine, this section will introduce you to a few terms and concepts designed to provide you with a very basic understanding of wine.

I. Cooking with Wine

What wine should we add to the recipe? This is a good question and one that rarely comes up when discussing wine. However, there are a great number of reasons to ask this question. For now, let's answer that question with a strong recommendation: only cook with a wine you would drink!

Do not use "cooking wines." Most cooking wines are made from poor quality base wine with salt and food coloring added. If you choose to ignore this suggestion, be sure to reduce the amount of salt you add to a recipe. Do not use wines that don't taste good to you, because they won't taste good in the recipe. Julia Child once stated, "If you do not have a good wine to use, it is far better to omit it, for a poor one can spoil a simple dish and utterly debase a noble one." Remember, though, price is not  always indicative of good taste. Many inexpensive wines are excellent to cook with.

Wine is so versatile; it can be used as a seasoning to add flavor to a dish, as a tenderizer for tougher cuts of meat and more. In this book you will find that every recipe includes wine as an ingredient. So decide on what fabulous dish you want to create, select the appropriate wine for the recipe and sip on a glass for inspiration as you prepare it. When cooking with wine, you will find that most of the alcohol evaporates during the cooking process. In fact, the alcohol in wine begins to evaporate at 172°F, well below the 212°F boiling point for water. As the alcohol disappears, so does the majority of calories, leaving only the concentrated flavors of the wine.

II. Types of Wine

Below you will find wine classified by basic styles, or vinification methods. This will help you decide where to begin when selecting the wine that is right for you or your recipe.

White – This wine is produced from white or black grapes that have had the skins removed before fermentation. Color may range from virtually colorless to yellow-green to amber. You will often see a green tinge in young white wines. White wines are best served well chilled.

Rosé – "Rosé" is French for "pink". This light, fresh and fruity wine is generally made from red grapes and can be either sweet, medium or dry. Color ranges from coral to pink to light red. This lighter color occurs when the grape skins are removed after fermentation begins. In the 1980s, "blush wines" were introduced. Beginning with White Zinfandel in California, they became the rage and their popularity has surpassed Rosés in the United States. These wines should be chilled before serving.

Red – Black grapes are fermented with the skin and pips (seeds) to make this wine. Color can range from deep purple to red to amber.

Fortified – Spirit (alcohol) has been added to these wines to increase their natural strength. For example, brandy is added to Sherry and Port. These wines can vary in color from a light brown to a deep purple and are normally sweeter than other red wines.

Sparkling – Sparkling wines are those with carbon dioxide that occurs either from fermentation or is added later. Amount of bubbles varies from slight to that of Champagne. To make Champagne, a yeast and sugar solution is added to dry table wine and then it is sealed for secondary fermentation.

In general, the wines above can be classified as "sweet", "dry"or some variation thereof. The difference between sweet and dry wines is the perceptible level of sugar in a wine. The tip of the tongue is where you have taste buds for recognizing sugar. Do you notice a sweet sensation when you taste the wine? Sweet indicates the presence of residual sugar, retained when grape sugar is not completely converted to alcohol. The opposite of sweet is dry. Dry wine usually has less than .5% residual sugar. Semi-dry and semi-sweet wines have sugar levels that fall somewhere in between. Most people take a while to acquire a taste for dry wine, which may be the reason some people feel they appear more sophisticated if they drink dry wine. The truth is, if you like a wine that is less sweet, go for a dry wine and if you like a sweet wine, then order it.

III. Understanding the Wine Bottle Label

1.) Grape Variety
2.) Appellation or
      Growing Region
3.) Vintage
4.) Producer Name
5.) Bottle Volume
6.) Alcohol Content

How do we know if the wine is any good? A good place to start is the wine label. Reading wine labels is part of the fun of learning about wine. The more information you have, the better your chances are of making a good purchasing decision. As Michael Broadbent once stated, "A sight of the label is worth 50 years experience."

The label on a bottle of wine undergoes considerable regulatory and creative scrutiny and contains information required by various governmental agencies. You can trust the label to be accurate. Domestic wine labels usually feature an attractive graphic and contain the following information, although some of the information may be on the second (back) label.

Grape Variety – This is a good indicator of how the wine will taste. Most countries require that at least 75% of the wine is made from the named grape variety. The appellation or region is more important to European winemakers, which is why the variety is often not listed on their labels.

Appellation or Growing Region – Appellation refers to the geographic location where the grapes were grown and is another good indicator of taste for that particular varietal (biological variety). Certain appellations' soil and climate are more conducive to producing a particular grape. Wine appellations may be as narrowly defined as a vineyard or as broadly defined as a country. Burgundy, Napa Valley and Mendoza are examples of appellations.

Producer Name – An identifying brand name and city are required on all bottles. This is usually the name of the winery, whether it be a small grower who makes and bottles their own wine or a large corporation that merely bottles the wine.

Alcohol Content – Wineries must list the amount of alcohol present in their wines. This can be listed as the degree of alcohol present (13.5 degrees) or the percent of alcohol present (13.5%). Alcohol content for table wine can range from a low of 7% to a high of 14%. You will find alcohol levels as high as 21% in fortified wines. Wineries are allowed a 1.5% leeway in the accuracy of the alcohol level.

Vintage Dating – A vineyard may produce great wine one year and poor wine the next. Some years are better than others and a vintage year may be listed on a U.S. wine label when 85% of the wine comes from grapes harvested and fermented within that calendar year.*

Quantity of Contents – Effective January 1, 1979, the U.S. Congress mandated that the wine industry use metric size bottles as the industry standard. A traditional wine bottle holds 750 ml (25.4 fluid ounces) of wine.

Legal Wording – Wine producers have been approved to include calorie, carbohydrate and protein content information on their label. This information will be seen on more and more bottles in the future.

Since November 18, 1989, any alcoholic beverage bottled or imported for sale in the U.S. must have a health warning from the Surgeon General listed on it. Also, any wine bottled after July 9, 1987, must include that it contains sulfites.

European wine labels are similar to those in the U.S., however there is no single standard. Perhaps the reason why is because every wine is a product of its history and terrior, which makes it unique.

IV. Learning to Taste Wine

Our first rule of wine tasting is to let your personal preferences guide you. The best wine will be the wine that tastes best to you. In the end, your opinion is the only one that matters.

Our second rule of wine tasting is to be open to trying varied types of wine. By following this rule, you may discover wonderful and delicious new flavors. In time, you will come to appreciate the delicacies and fine nuances that wine offers.

To fully enjoy the wine tasting ritual, the following ideas can help you prepare:

1. Remove heavy cologne or lipstick. Strong fragrances can distort the smell of the wine and lipstick may impact the taste.

2. Avoid food or drink that can impair taste such as garlic, raw onions, or vinegar. Brushing your teeth or chewing on a breath mint or gum will also impact taste. If needed, cleanse your palate with bland cheese, salt-free bread or an unsalted cracker.

3. Prepare the wine for tasting. Red wines need to have the corks removed so they can "breathe" for a period of time before tasting. White wines will need to be chilled.

4. Pour the wine into a wine glass. Only a small amount is needed for tasting.

5. Now relax and prepare to enjoy the experience. You need to take your time when you taste wine.

Tasting wine requires that you use your senses:

Look – Examine the color and clarity of the wine. You will want wine with clear, appropriate color. Reds may have some sediment that will settle to the bottom when you let the wine breathe. They should have a dark, ruby color that will darken with age. Whites also grow darker as they age. Whites that have a darker red or brown color may have passed their prime and gone bad. "Colour is like a wine's face. From it you can tell age, and something of character." Emile Peynaud

Smell – Place the bottom of your glass on a table and gently rotate so that it swirls the wine in the glass. This will add oxygen to the wine and release the aroma and bouquet of the wine, known as the "nose". Hold the glass to your nose and sniff. Do you smell a flower, fruit, spice, herb, nut or other substance? If you smell flowers in the wine, one may say the wine has a flowery nose. Does the wine have a good nose (pleasant smell) or an off-nose (unpleasant odor)? Wine tasters know that smell is important. Much of what we believe we taste actually comes through our noses.

Taste and Feel – Take a sip of the wine and hold it in you mouth for several seconds. Swish it around as you draw air in and then swallow (or spit it out). Did you feel the lightness or weight of the wine? Wines will range from watery-thin to viscous and oily. You want a wine that is well balanced. Can you taste a variety of flavors? Does the wine have the right amount of sweetness or acidity?

Reflect – Think about the wine you just tasted. You may want to close your eyes to remove any visual distractions. The taste that lingers in your mouth after swallowing is called the finish. Does the taste end right away (short finish) or does it remain rich and smooth (firm finish) after swallowing? Once you have had a chance to reflect on it, you are ready to talk about it. Much can be learned by discussing the wine with those around you. "When you taste don't look at the bottle, nor the label, nor your surroundings, but look directly inwards to yourself, to observe sensations at their birth and develop impressions to remember." Pierre Poupon

V. Pairing Wine with Food

If you research articles from years ago, you will find they listed hard and fast rules about what wine to serve with a meal. "White wine with chicken or fish. Red wine with beef." People will tell you that those rules no longer apply. The new rule has become, "If you like it, serve it with anything." The authors agree with this sentiment.

Each recipe in this book will call out a suggested wine to use as an ingredient. After preparing some of these, you will begin to sense how to select an interesting taste complement for your own recipes. Below are some suggestions to help you determine which wine to add to your favorite recipe. **This list is by no means exhaustive.** And, don't forget to pour the chef a glass of your chosen wine to enjoy while preparing the meal!

Menu Item	Cooking Group	Wine Recommendation
Fish, shellfish, poultry, pork and veal	Dry white wine	Sauvignon Blanc, Chardonnay
Poultry, vegetable soups	Dry, fortified wine	Sherry
Seafood soups, light/cream sauces	Off-dry white wine	Riesling
Red meat, red sauces	Young, full-bodied, red wine	Pinot Noir
Soups with root vegetables and/or beef	Earthy, full-bodied, red wine	Merlot, Cabernet Sauvignon
Sweet desserts	Sweet white wine or sweet fortified wine	Port
Local cuisine	Local wine	Local wine

VI. Ordering Wine at a Restaurant

"Please don't put me in charge of selecting the wine! What if I pick the wrong one?"

If you have ever felt this way, you are not alone. The good news is that the process for ordering wine at a restaurant is based on traditions, and the only requirement for the diner is to sit and wait for the wine to be poured. With this is mind, let's walk through the process.

Any quality restaurant will have a wine captain or sommelier to help you choose the right wine. It is definitely appropriate to ask for their help. With their guidance, you can feel confident about the decision you make.

After you have chosen the wine, the waiter will bring out the bottle and show you the label. This is done to ensure the customer that they are getting the exact wine they ordered. Quickly verify that it is the wine and vintage you selected

At this point the waiter will open the wine in front of you. The reason the wine is uncorked in front of you is to reassure you that the restaurant is not substituting an inexpensive wine for the wine you ordered.

Once the cork has been removed, the waiter will offer it to you for inspection. All you need to do is set it down on the table. The purpose of presenting the cork to the customer is so they can see that the cork is intact and moist at the end that was next to the wine.

Next the waiter will pour a small amount of wine into your glass. Make sure the wine is clear and has good color. Now swirl it, sniff it, sip it and give the waiter a nod if you like it. At this point the waiter will fill the glasses around the table, finishing with your glass.

You are done! The key is to remember that ordering wine at a restaurant should be fun, so loosen up and enjoy. Now, experiment with some wines you have never tried before!

In 2006, the Alcohol and Tobacco Tax and Trade Bureau (TTB) made a ruling that brought American wines in line with 85% standard in other wine-producing countries. The 95% standard is still in place for wine with a single American viticultural area (or its foreign equivalent.)

THE GREAT WINE PYRAMID

GRAINS

BASIL LEMON FARFALLE AND SHRIMP

Difficulty: ♟♟♟
Preparation Time: 45 minutes
Yield: 6 servings

4 quarts water
3 tablespoons salt
1 1/2 pounds shrimp, shelled and deveined
2 tablespoons pickling spice
1/2 cup unsalted butter
1/4 cup Chenin Blanc
Juice and zest from one large lemon
1 tablespoon minced shallots
2 teaspoons minced garlic
2 cups cream
3/4 cup grated Parmesan cheese
1/2 teaspoon salt, or more to taste
4 quarts boiling water
2 tablespoons salt
1 pound farfalle pasta
1 tablespoon finely minced basil

1. Add 3 tablespoons salt to 4 quarts of water. Bring to a boil. Add shrimp and pickling spices; return to a boil and cook until shrimp turn pink and curl.

2. Pour shrimp into colander and wash off pickling spices. Drain well.

3. Melt butter in saucepan with wine, lemon zest and juice. Add shallots and garlic. Cook until soft. Add cream and Parmesan cheese, whisking to emulsify. Add salt to taste. Turn off heat.

4. In pot of boiling water add 2 tablespoons salt and stir until dissolved. Add pasta and cook until tender. Drain into colander.

5. Combine shrimp and pasta with cream sauce and fold in basil. Heat slowly and serve.

Contributed by Susan Auler of Fall Creek Vineyards

CHEESY RICE

Difficulty: ❢
Preparation Time: 40 minutes
Yield: 6 servings

1/3 cup green pepper, finely chopped
1/2 cup green onion, chopped
3/4 cup long grain white rice, uncooked
3 tablespoons butter
1 1/2 teaspoons salt
16-ounce can diced tomatoes
1/2 cup dry white wine
1 cup cubed cheddar cheese

1. In a Dutch oven, heat butter and sauté green pepper, onions and rice over medium heat until rice is lightly browned.

2. Add salt, tomatoes and wine. Cook, covered, over low heat until rice is tender and liquid is absorbed, about 25 minutes.

3. Stir in cubed cheese. Remove from heat, cover and let stand until cheese begins to melt, about 5 minutes.

Quite a few estates of famous "dead" celebrities are generating income from licensing the celebrity's name and image. A few well-known examples include:

In 1985, Marilyn Wines began production of Marilyn Merlot. Acclaim from critics, collectors and lovers of fine wine led to the production of additional wines including Marilyn Cabernet and Norma Jeane wines.

Elvis Presley wines by Graceland Cellars, including "Jailhouse Red" and "Blue Suede Chardonnay" can be found in retail stores across the nation.

The Jerry Garcia Estate in Sonoma County, named for lead guitarist and composer for the Grateful Dead and Jerry Garcia Band, released their first wines in 2003.

BUZZ ON THE VINE

Have you every wondered how the practice of offering a toast began? The word *toast* originated with the Romans. They would lay a piece of burnt bread in their wine glass, allowing the charcoal to reduce the acidity of the wine and make it more drinkable. Over time, the word *toast* (*tostus* in Latin) came to define a tradition of raising your glass to honor someone.

By the 18th century, toasting had become very popular at parties and various other functions. Toasts were made to anyone and everyone. Research tells us that beautiful women to whom toasts were made, became known as the "toast of the town". By the 19th century, it was considered rude if a host didn't toast their guests.

Today, toasts are a special gesture which allows us to compliment or shower appreciation on someone else. Below are a few hints for giving a good toast:

1. The best toasts are simple, short and to the point.
2. Know your audience. Match the toast to the honoree and guests in attendance. Try not to offend anyone.
3. Stand up to give the toast with your glass raised.
4. Begin by introducing your relationship to the honoree, if appropriate.
5. Share a humorous or positive story about the honoree or quote a famous line.
6. A heart-felt comment can be very impactful.
7. When possible, prepare and practice the toast ahead of time.
8. Finish the toast on a positive note, raise your glass slightly higher and say, "Cheers!"

Receiving a toast is easy. Do not drink to the toast or stand. Once the toast has been given, simply stand to acknowledge the giver with a gesture or comment of your own.

Throughout this book, you will find several of our favorite toasts included. You can easily locate them by looking for the frog icon in this feature.

"May your glass be ever full,
May the roof over your head be always strong.
And may you be in heaven half an hour
Before the devil knows you're dead."
– Old Irish Toast

T ake the opportunity to pay tribute to friends and family by giving memorable toasts.
CHEERS!

CELLAR CHALLENGE

Can you match the movies with the memorable quotes below?

a. *Sideways*
b. *Batman Forever*
c. *Goldfinger*
d. *It's a Wonderful Life*
e. *The Jerk*

f. *Never Give a Sucker an Even Break*
g. *The Three Musketeers*
h. *The Muppet Movie*
i. *The Silence of the Lambs*
j. *Dracula: Dead and Loving It*

_____ 1. "Bread — that this house may never know hunger. Salt — that life may always have flavor. Wine — that joy and prosperity may reign forever."

_____ 2. "Ah. Fortune smiles. Another day of wine and roses. Or, in your case, beer and pizza!"

_____ 3. "A census taker once tried to test me. I ate his liver with some fava beans and a nice Chianti."

_____ 4. "Ah yes — but no more 1966. Let's splurge! Bring us some fresh wine! The freshest you've got — this year! No more of this old stuff."

_____ 5. "The picnic was delicious, the wine was excellent, remind me to send the Cardinal a note."

_____ 6. "I'm drinking wine...and eating chicken! And it's good!"

_____ 7. "Mmm. A little citrus. Maybe some strawberry. Mmm. Passion fruit. Mmm. And — ah, there's just, like, the faintest … soupçon of like, uh, asparagus and there's a — just a flutter of, like, a — like a nutty Edam cheese."

_____ 8. "My dear girl, there are some things that just aren't done, such as drinking Dom Perignon '53 above the temperature of 38 degrees Fahrenheit. That's just as bad as listening to the Beatles without earmuffs!"

_____ 9. "Sparkling Muscatel. One of the finest wines of Idaho."

_____ 10. "I was in love with a beautiful blonde once. She drove me to drink; that's the one thing I'm indebted to her for."

Solutions on page 240

CHERRY PANCAKES

This age-old German recipe, also known as Kirschpfannkuchen, is delicious with typical breakfast, brunch or lunch fare.

Difficulty: ♟♟
Preparation Time: 40 minutes
Yield: 6 servings

4 medium-sized French dinner rolls
Water
2 eggs
1/4 cup flour, sifted
2 teaspoons sugar
1/2 teaspoon salt
1/2 cup milk
1/2 cup dry red wine
3-pound can tart, pitted cherries, drained
5 tablespoons butter
1/2 cup sugar
1 tablespoon ground cinnamon

1. Blend 1/2 cup sugar with cinnamon to make cinnamon sugar. Set aside.

2. In a bowl, soak rolls with enough water to cover. In a separate bowl, beat eggs lightly. Add flour, sugar, salt, milk and wine and blend until smooth.

3. Squeeze the rolls dry and then crumble them into the egg mixture. Fold in the cherries.

4. Melt butter in a skillet or griddle. Drop the batter, from your spoon, into the heated butter in rounds about 1 1/2-inches in diameter. Cook as you would normal pancakes until crisp and golden on one side. Flip carefully to do the same on the other side.

5. Serve warm, sprinkled with cinnamon sugar and butter or syrup.

CHESTNUT POULTRY STUFFING

Difficulty: 🍷🍷
Preparation Time: 30 minutes
Yield: Enough to stuff a 15-pound turkey

1/2 pound butter
1 large onion, chopped
4 cups celery including leaves, chopped coarsely
1/4 cup parsley, chopped
6 cups dry white bread cubes
1 pound roasted chestnuts, chopped
Salt and pepper to taste
1/8 teaspoon nutmeg
1/4 cup half-and-half
1/3 cup dry white wine

1. In a skillet, heat butter and sauté the onion, celery and parsley, stirring, for 8 minutes.

2. In a large bowl, combine bread cubes, chestnuts, salt, pepper and nutmeg. Toss to mix well.

3. In another bowl, combine half-and-half and wine then add to the bread mixture. Add the vegetables (along with pan dripping) to the mixture. Toss all together and stuff into turkey cavity.

> " . . . I like to think about what was going on the year the grapes were growing; how the sun was shining; if it rained. I like to think about all the people who tended and picked the grapes. And if it's an old wine, how many of them must be dead by now. I like how wine continues to evolve, like if I opened a bottle of wine today it would taste different than if I'd opened it on any other day, because a bottle of wine is actually alive. And it's constantly evolving and gaining complexity. That is, until it peaks, like your '61. And then it begins its steady, inevitable decline."
> ~Maya, from the movie *Sideways*

wine wit

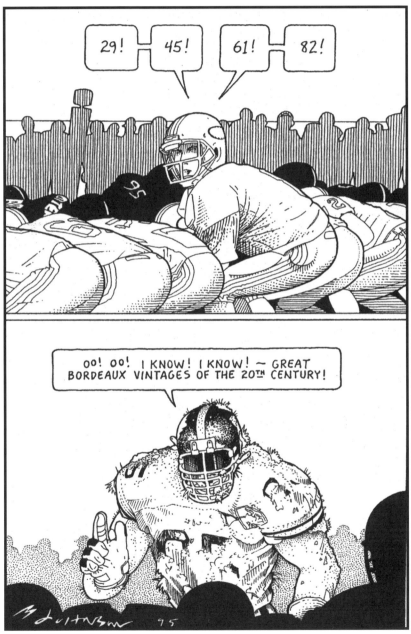

MACARONI CASSEROLE

Enjoy this microwave-easy twist on an old favorite with salad and crusty bread.

Difficulty: 🍷🍷
Preparation Time: 25 minutes
Yield: 4-6 servings

8 ounces macaroni
1/4 cup butter or margarine
1 onion, finely chopped
1 garlic clove, finely crushed
1/2 cup bell pepper, diced
1/2 cup fresh mushrooms, sliced
14-ounce can diced tomatoes, drained
1/4 cup tomato paste
8 ounces ham or bacon, cooked and finely chopped
1/2 cup dry white wine
Ground black pepper
Garnishes: chopped parsley, grated Parmesan, crushed red pepper
  (all optional)

1. In a large saucepan, cook macaroni in salted water until al dente. Drain and keep warm.

2. Meanwhile, in a 3 quart casserole, melt the butter or margarine in a microwave. Stir the onion and garlic into the butter and cook, covered on high for 2 minutes.

3. Stir in the pepper, mushrooms, tomatoes, tomato paste, ham or bacon, wine and black pepper. Cook on high 5 minutes.

4. Stir the pasta into the tomato mixture. Cover and heat on medium-high for 4 minutes or until warmed through. Top with garnishes if desired.

WineWisdom

"Wine in moderation . . . brightens the eye, improves the voice, imparts a new vivacity to one's thoughts and conversation."
~Charles Dickens~

"A man will be eloquent if you give him good wine."
~Ralph Waldo Emerson~

"What contemptible scoundrel stole the cork from my lunch?"
~W. C. Fields~

"Quickly bring me a beaker of wine, so that I may wet my wits and say something clever."
~Aristophanes~

"Go thy way, eat thy bread with joy, and drink thy wine with a merry heart."
~Ecclesiastes 9:7~

"Excellent wine generates enthusiasm. And whatever you do with enthusiasm is generally successful."
~Phillippe de Rothschild~

"Three glasses of wine can set everything to rights."
~Chinese Proverb~

"Ha! Ha! Ha! I'm full of wine, heavy with joy divine."
~Percy Bysshe Shelley~

"The rapture of drinking and wine's dizzy joy no man who is sober deserves."
~Li Po~

"This wine should be eaten; it is too good to be drunk."
~Jonathan Swift~

MUSTARD DILL BISCUITS

Difficulty: 🍷🍷
Preparation Time: 35 minutes
Yield: 12 biscuits

1 1/2 cups flour
2/3 cup oatmeal
2 tablespoons sugar
1 teaspoon salt
3 teaspoons baking powder
2 tablespoons sesame seeds
1 tablespoon dill (dry or fresh)
8 tablespoons butter
2 tablespoons Chenin Blanc Mustard
3/4 cup milk

1. Heat oven to 350°. Lightly oil cookie sheet.

2. Combine all dry ingredients. Cut in butter until pea size chunks remain.

3. Add milk and mustard to dry ingredients. Mix until dough just comes together.

4. Roll into a ball and pat out to be 1-inch thick. Use cutter (approximately 1 3/4-inches for best results) to make biscuits. Pat dough together again and cut until no dough remains.

5. Bake for 12 to 15 minutes or until golden brown.

Contributed by Susan Auler of Fall Creek Vineyards

PATTY CLAIR'S MACARONI PARISIEN

Difficulty: ♟♟♟

Preparation Time: 45 minutes

Yield: 4 servings

4 chicken breasts
1/4 pound butter
1/4 cup Madeira
2 tablespoons flour
2 cups chicken broth
1 cup cream
1 cup grated Parmesan cheese
Salt and pepper
3/4 cup cooked ham or prosciutto
1 pound ziti

1. Heat oven to 350°.

2. Sauté chicken breasts in 4-6 tablespoons butter. Cook about 10 minutes. Pour Madeira over the chicken breasts and let it cook down for a few seconds. Remove the chicken and save the juices.

3. Prepare sauce with 2 tablespoons butter, flour and chicken broth. Add pan juices, cream and grated Parmesan. Blend well and season with salt and pepper.

4. Cut chicken and ham or prosciutto into a fine julienne.

5. In boiling, salted water, cook ziti until al dente. Drain, and then combine with the cream sauce and meat.

6. Spoon all into an ovenproof baking dish. Sprinkle with grated Parmesan and bake for 15 minutes.

WINE WORDS

Part One: *Terms used when wine tasting and drinking*:

❦ *Aftertaste* – Also called the "finish", this refers to the impression that a wine leaves in your mouth after it is swallowed: not only the flavors, but how long the taste lingers.

❦ *Aroma* – This word is used to describe the smells directly related to the wine grape, usually used to indicate floral or spicy smells. It is often said that young wines have aroma and aged wines have bouquet.

❦ *Astringent* – Tannins from the grape skins, seeds and oak leave a drying taste in the mouth. You can detect an excess of tannins or astringency by a puckering of your mouth as the tannins hit your taste buds.

❦ *Balance* – When no single element of the wine overpowers another, it is said to be balanced or integrated. Those components include fruit, acidity, tannins and alcohol.

❦ *Big* – Tasters often use this term when describing a wine that is full of flavor and contains high levels of grape flavor, tannins and alcohol.

❦ *Body* – This is how you perceive the weight and texture of the wine in your mouth, which is predominantly determined by its alcohol strength. A wine can be light, medium or full bodied.

❦ *Bouquet* – Referring to the smells that are given off from a wine when opened. It is a complex combination of the aromas that come from the fruit and alcohol as it ages or ferments.

❦ *Breathe* – When you open a wine and allow it to mix with air to develop its flavors. This is important to do with red wines before serving them.

❦ *Continued on Page 34*

PEANUT BUTTER AND CHUTNEY CANAPÉS

Difficulty: ♟

Preparation time: 15 minutes

Yield: 2 cups

1 cup chunky peanut butter
4 ounces soft cream cheese
1/4 teaspoon seasoned salt
1/3 cup Burgundy or other dry red wine
1/2 teaspoon Worcestershire sauce
1 1/2 cups Major Grey's chutney, diced
1 loaf egg or rye bread, sliced and toasted

1. Blend all ingredients except the bread.

2. Spread on toast and cut into decorative triangles or fingers.

RASPBERRY MUFFINS
Difficulty: ♟♟
Preparation Time: 40 minutes
Yield: 18 muffins

1 cup butter
1 cup sugar
2 large eggs
3 cups all-purpose flour
1/8 tablespoon double-acting baking powder
1/2 teaspoon salt
1/8 teaspoon baking soda
1 cup raspberry wine
1 teaspoon vanilla
1/2 cup minced fresh raspberries

1. Heat oven to 400°. Grease muffin pan.

2. In a large bowl, cream together the butter and sugar until the mixture is light and fluffy. Beat in the eggs one at a time.

3. In a separate bowl sift together flour, baking powder, salt and baking soda (reserve 3 tablespoons flour).

4. Stir together raspberry wine and vanilla. Add the 3 tablespoons of flour to the fresh raspberries and mix.

5. Stir all together into the muffin mixture. Spoon batter into a greased muffin pan. Bake for 25 minutes.

Contributed by Bargetto Winery

RICE SALAD WITH SHERRY DRESSING

Difficulty: ♟♟

Preparation time: 20 minutes plus cooling time

Yield: 8 servings

4 1/2 cups cooked white rice, cooled to room temperature
2 medium carrots, sliced diagonally
1/2 cup cooking oil
1/3 cup dry Sherry
1 small, yellow squash, chopped
1 cup broccoli flowerets
10 cherry tomatoes, halved
1/4 cup radishes, thinly sliced
1/4 cup cider vinegar
1 garlic clove, minced
1 teaspoon sugar

1. In a skillet, heat 1 teaspoon of the oil and 1 teaspoon of the Sherry. Add carrots and cook for 2 minutes, stirring frequently.

2. Add squash and broccoli and cook 2 more minutes, stirring frequently.

3. In a large salad bowl, combine cooked rice, carrot mixture, tomatoes and radishes. Mix well.

4. In a separate bowl, combine remaining oil and Sherry, vinegar, garlic and sugar. Mix well. Add to salad and mix well.

5. Chill, covered, for several hours before serving.

A unique and memorable gift for a young child is birth year wine. Give a nice bottle of wine that can be consumed for a 21st birthday or other significant occasion. Most of the long-aging wines are released about 2-3 years after the birth/vintage year, so this makes a wonderful 3rd birthday gift. White wines, sparkling wines and most red wines will go bad long before the special occasion. For this reason, we recommend giving a big red wine or dessert wine, such as a Vintage Port.

WINEWISDOM

"A waltz and a glass of wine can invite an encore."
~Johann Strauss~

"I cook with wine; sometimes I even add it to the food."
~W. C. Fields~

"There is no substitute for pulling corks."
~Alexis Lichine~

"[Wine] is the professor of taste, the liberator of the spirit, and the light of intelligence."
~Paul Claudel~

"Within the bottle's depths, the wine's soul sang one night."
~Charles Baudelaire~

"There are two reasons for drinking; one is, when you are thirsty, to cure it; the other, when you are not thirsty, to prevent it."
~Thomas Love Peacock~

"With a dear friend, a thousand cups of wine are too few."
~Chinese Proverb~

"I feast on wine and bread, and feasts they are."
~Michelangelo~

"Wine can of their wits the wise beguile, make the sage frolic, and the serious smile."
~Homer~

"Water separates the people of the world, wine unites them."
~Anonymous~

SHARI'S SIGNATURE LASAGNA
Difficulty: ❦❦❦❦
Preparation Time: 4 hours
Yield: 8 servings

1 pound ground meat
1 large onion, diced
3 cloves garlic, crushed
1 tablespoon oregano
1/2 cup red table wine
1/2 pound mushrooms. chopped
1/2 pound pepperoni, chopped
1 large can tomato paste
1 large can tomato sauce
1 pound mozzarella
1 pound ricotta
1 pound lasagna noodles
Grated Parmesan cheese

1. Brown ground meat in a large Dutch oven. Add onion, garlic and oregano. Continue to cook on low for 10 minutes.

2. Add tomato paste, tomato sauce, wine, mushrooms, pepperoni and water if needed. Simmer sauce covered for 2 1/2 hours.

3. Approximately 30 minutes before sauce is done, cook noodles according to package directions. Slice the mozzarella thinly.

4. Heat oven to 350°.

5. In a large casserole pan, layer in the following order: meat sauce, noodles, ricotta and mozzarella. Repeat. Top with grated Parmesan and bake for 1 hour.

SIMPLY WONDERFUL WINE BISCUITS

Difficulty: ♈♈

Preparation Time: 45 minutes

Yield: 2 dozen

2 1/2 cups all-purpose flour
1/3 cup white sugar
2 1/2 teaspoons baking powder
1/2 teaspoon salt
1 egg
1/2 cup vegetable oil
1/3 cup Dolcetto wine or Zinfandel
1 egg white
2 tablespoons sesame seeds, toasted

1. Preheat the oven to 325°. Grease cookie sheets.

2. In a medium bowl, stir together the flour, sugar, baking powder and salt.

3. Add the egg, oil and wine all at once and mix until well blended. Let the dough rest for 5 minutes.

4. Roll the dough into log shapes and cut into irregularly shaped 1- inch slices.

5. Roll each piece of dough in the egg white and then roll to coat with sesame seeds.

6. Place biscuits at least 1-inch apart onto the prepared cookie sheets.

7. Bake for 25 to 30 minutes in the preheated oven, until lightly browned. Turn the oven off and leave the biscuits inside to crisp. These biscuits will keep for weeks in an airtight container.

Contributed by Callaway Vineyard and Winery

wine wit

THE JUGS MOVE IN

STEAK DIJON SANDWICHES

Difficulty: ▼▼
Preparation Time: 25 minutes
Yield: 4 servings

1 1/2 pounds top round steak, 1-inch thick
2 tablespoons butter or margarine
1/4 teaspoon salt
1/4 teaspoon garlic salt
1/4 teaspoon onion salt
1 teaspoon beef broth
1 1/2 teaspoons Dijon-style mustard
1/2 cup Cabernet Sauvignon
1 tablespoon chives, chopped
1 tablespoon parsley, chopped
8 thick slices of French bread, toasted

1. Cut steak into four even pieces. In a skillet, melt butter and pan fry the steaks over medium-high heat approximately 8 minutes, turning to brown on both sides.

2. Season steaks with the salts. Remove from pan and keep warm.

3. Add broth, mustard and wine to the pan. Cook on high heat until volume reduces by half.

4. Assemble sandwiches by layering the bottom bread slice with a steak, sauce and sprinkled chives and parsley. Top with another bread slice.

When you hold a Champagne bottle upside down, you will see an indentation on the bottom. What is this indentation called?
a. bubble
b. trough
c. valley
d. punt

Solution: d. The "push-up" on the bottom is called a punt.

WILD MUSHROOM RISOTTO

Difficulty: 🍷🍷
Preparation Time: 30 minutes
Yield: 4 servings

2 teaspoons olive oil
1 clove garlic, minced
1 cup Arborio rice
2 2/3 cups chicken broth
8 ounces wild mushrooms, diced
1 ounce Parmesan cheese, grated
1 ounce Blanco Grande or other dry white wine

1. Heat oil and sauté garlic until tender but not brown.

2. Add rice. Stir until opaque, about 3 to 4 minutes.

3. Add mushrooms and 2/3 cup of the broth. Bring to a boil. Reduce heat and continue stirring.

4. When liquid is absorbed, add another 2/3 cup of the broth. Stir. Continue this process until all broth has been absorbed.

5. When rice is done, remove from heat. Stir in the Parmesan cheese and wine.

Contributed by Chef Dana Taylor of Los Pinos Ranch Vineyards

*"May the people who dance on your grave,
Get cramps in their legs."
-From the book, The Joys of Yiddish*

Buzz on the Vine

The Hebrew word kosher means "fit for use" and is used to designate foods with ingredients and manufacturing processes acceptable to Jewish dietary laws. The roots of kosher law or "kashrut" come from the Torah (also known as the Old Testament of the Bible) where God laid out his regulations for what Jews may and may not consume. Below are key requirements for a kosher wine:

- The wine must be made by Sabbath observant Jews.
- The equipment used can only be used for making kosher wines.
- Only certified kosher ingredients can be used.
- No artificial coloring or preservatives can be used.

If a non-Jew handles the wine, from grape crushing to consumption, then it is no longer considered kosher. The exception to this rule is when a wine has been pasteurized. Flash pasteurization involves heating the wine to near boiling and then cooling in a flash. Wines that have gone through this process are called "mevushal" and you will find them marked as such on the bottle. Mevushal wine allows Jews and non-Jews to be present and handle it, which is why it is commonly found at weddings and other celebrations.

Over the years, kosher wine has been synonymous with sweet, syrupy wine. The past 20 years however, have seen tremendous growth in variety, quality and scope of kosher wines. As the taste of kosher wine continues to improve, so will the numbers of those who enjoy it.

"Blessed are Thou, O Lord our God, King of the Universe, Creator of the fruit of the vine."
Traditional Hebrew blessing over wine

VEGETABLES

ARTICHOKE DIP

Difficulty: 🍷
Preparation Time: 40 minutes
Yield: 16 appetizer servings

9 ounces artichoke hearts, drained and chopped
1 cup mayonnaise
1/2 cup Sauvignon Blanc or other light white wine
1 cup grated Parmesan cheese
1/2 cup plain bread crumbs
1/4 teaspoon white pepper
1/4 teaspoon oregano
Crackers

1. Heat oven to 350°.

2. Add wine to mayonnaise and blend well. Blend in artichokes, cheese, bread crumbs, pepper and oregano.

3. Bake in an ungreased pan for 30 minutes.

4. Serve atop buttery crackers.

BABY ARTICHOKES PROVENÇAL

Difficulty: ♟♟♟

Preparation Time: 50 minutes

Yield: 6 servings

18 baby artichokes
1/2 cup best-quality olive oil
3 large carrots, peeled and cut into small dice
3 leeks (white part and 3-inches green), well rinsed, dried, and chopped
4 cloves garlic, minced
Salt and freshly ground black pepper, to taste
1/2 cup dry white wine
1 tablespoon fresh lemon juice
4 ounces Montrachet or other soft mild chèvre cheese
Nicoise or Ligurian olives, for garnish

1. Cut the stem and 1/4-inch of the top from each artichoke. Trim the tough outer leaves with scissors.

2. Heat the oil in a saucepan large enough to hold all the artichokes upright over medium-high heat. Add the carrots, leeks, and garlic and sauté, stirring frequently, for 10 minutes. Season to taste with salt and lots of black pepper.

3. Place the artichokes upright on the bed of vegetables and pour in the wine. Sprinkle the lemon juice over the tops of the artichokes. Cover the pan and simmer over medium-low heat for 20 to 25 minutes. Remove from heat and cool to room temperature.

4. Remove the artichokes from the vegetables and set aside. Crumble the chèvre into the vegetable mixture and fold gently together. Spoon the vegetable mixture onto a platter or 6 individual serving plates. Arrange the artichokes on top of the vegetables, spooning a few vegetables over the tops. If you are serving on plates, allow 3 artichokes per serving. Garnish with olives and serve at room temperature.

Contributed by Andretti Winery

BEETS WITH MANDARIN ORANGES

Difficulty: ♟♟

Preparation Time: 30 minutes

Yield: 8 servings

1/3 cup sugar
1 1/2 teaspoons cornstarch
2 tablespoons lemon juice
1/3 cup Chablis
2 tablespoons butter or margarine
11-ounce can mandarin oranges, drained
32 ounces canned small, whole beets, drained

1. Heat oven to 350°. Grease a 1 1/2-quart casserole dish.

2. In a saucepan, combine sugar and cornstarch. Add lemon juice and wine and stir until blended.

3. Add butter and cook over medium heat, stirring constantly until mixture boils, thickens and becomes clear. Remove from heat.

4. Combine drained beets and oranges in greased casserole dish. Pour the thickened sauce over them. Bake for 15 minutes or until heated through.

CELLAR CHALLENGE

Do you know your bubbly?

1. In Champagne country, Champagnes are named for the houses that produce them. Which was the first French Champagne house to open in California?
   - a.) Bollinger
   - b.) Moët et Chandon
   - c.) G. H. Mumm
   - d.) Louis Roederer

2. In 1970, the European Union banned the use of the word *Champagne* on sparkling wines produced outside of France. Spanish sparkling wines are now known as:
   - a.) Vinata
   - b.) Roblé
   - c.) Cava
   - d.) Nova

3. Sparkling wines from this country are called Sekt. You will find Rieslings used in their better wines.
   - a.) Finland
   - b.) Germany
   - c.) Sweden
   - d.) South Africa

4. How many bubbles are in a bottle of sparkling wine?
   - a.) 7 million
   - b.) 23 million
   - c.) 36 million
   - d.) 49 million

 Solutions on page 240

BLACK BEAN AND CORN TURKEY CHILI

This dish may be paired with a salad of mixed greens, avocado, mandarin oranges and toasted almonds.

Difficulty: ❢❢❢
Preparation Time: 40 minutes
Yield: 8 servings

2 tablespoons olive oil
2 medium onions, chopped
2 pounds ground turkey
1/2 teaspoon black pepper
1 teaspoon salt
8-ounce can diced green chilies
1 tablespoon dried oregano
1 tablespoon dried basil or 2-3 tablespoons chopped fresh basil
3 tablespoons chili powder
12-ounce can tomato paste
28-ounce can plum tomatoes, diced
3/4 cup Syrah
Two 16-ounce cans black beans, drained and rinsed well
Two 16-ounce cans sweet corn, drained and rinsed well
Grated cheddar cheese
Sour cream
Cilantro, chopped

1. Heat olive oil in a large covered pot and sauté onions over low heat until translucent and slightly brown. Add turkey and brown. Drain fat from pan.

2. Add pepper, salt, chilies, oregano, basil and chili powder. Add tomato paste and blend.

3. Add tomatoes, wine, beans and corn and simmer for 25 minutes. Adjust seasonings as necessary.

4. Serve with grated cheese, sour cream, chopped cilantro and Syrah.

Contributed by Firestone Vineyards

CAULIFLOWER MOUSSE

Difficulty: ♟♟♟♟
Preparation Time: 1 1/2 hours
Yield: 8 servings

1 1/2 cups water
2 cubes chicken bouillon
4 cups cauliflower flowerets
4 tablespoons butter
4 tablespoons flour
1 teaspoon salt
1 cup grated Swiss cheese
1/4 cup Sauvignon Blanc
4 eggs, separated
1 green onion, thinly sliced
1/2 cup half-and-half
Butter for coating soufflé dish

1. Heat oven to 375°. Butter a 2-quart soufflé dish.

2. Bring water to boil in medium saucepan. Add bouillon cubes, then cauliflower. Cook until tender.

3. Melt butter in separate large saucepan. Whisk in flour and salt until well blended.

4. Add 1/2 cup water from cooked cauliflower, stirring with whisk until thickened and smooth.

5. Add cheese and wine, blending well. Cool the mixture, then beat in one egg yolk at a time.

6. Put cauliflower, remaining bouillon liquid (1/2 cup), green onion and half-and-half in processor. Purée until smooth.

7. Add cauliflower mixture to flour mixture, combining well.

8. Beat egg whites until stiff but not dry. Carefully fold into cauliflower/flour mixture.

9. Pour into soufflé dish and bake 30-40 minutes until browned on top. Lay a piece of foil on top of soufflé dish and continue cooking 20 minutes more or until soufflé is firm. Serve immediately.

Contributed by Susan Auler of Fall Creek Vineyards

WINE WORDS

Part One "Tasting", Continued from Page 16:

 ♟ *Clarity* – This refers to the appearance of the wine and indicates whether or not it has any cloudiness in it. Tasters often hold a glass upwards towards the light to determine clarity.

 ♟ *Chewy* – A "big" wine that has noticeable tannins can be thought of as chewy.

 ♟ *Clean* – A refreshing wine that has no off-flavors or odors.

 ♟ *Coarse* – This is a term used for a wine without much interest and is ordinary or rough.

 ♟ *Complex* – As wines age they acquire many different flavor nuances that, when well merged, give a wine interest and personality and make it complex.

 ♟ *Corked* – Affecting about 3% of wines worldwide, this adjective is for a wine whose quality has been affected by a defective cork. These wines will have a moldy, rotten wood smell and bitter taste.

 ♟ *Crisp* – This term is used for a white wine that has refreshing acidity without much sweetness.

 ♟ *Delicate* – Describes a wine that is light-bodied and without strong flavor, yet well-balanced and pleasing.

 ♟ *Depth* – Describes wines that are intense and have complex flavors. These wines can also be called concentrated.

 ♟ *Dry* – When all sugars have been converted to alcohol, a wine is described as dry.

♟ *Continued on Page 68*

CHILLED CHAMPAGNE-CUCUMBER SOUP

Difficulty: 🍷🍷

Preparation Time: 30 minutes plus chilling time
Yield: 6 servings

2 English cucumbers, peeled and chopped
2 bunches green onions, chopped
2 tablespoons olive oil
2 tablespoons flour
1 quart vegetable stock
1 cup plain yogurt
1/2 cup Chardonnay Champagne
1 tablespoon fresh mint leaves, chopped
Salt and pepper, to taste
Extra cucumber slices and mint as garnish

1. Sauté cucumber and onion in olive oil until soft. Add flour and stir for 2-3 minutes. Add stock, salt and pepper. Simmer for 15 minutes.

2. Add yogurt, mint and Champagne. Remove from heat and pour into blender. Purée until smooth.

3. Chill completely before serving. Garnish with cucumber slices and mint.

Contributed by Chef Robin Lehnhoff of Korbel Champagne Cellars

35

Buzz on the Vine

One would think that the hottest debate in the wine world would be about vintages, varietals and appellations. It's not. The biggest debate concerns how to seal a bottle of wine: cork or screw cap.

Cork comes from the cork tree, Quercus Suber, a species of oak tree that grows in Portugal and Spain. Wooden corks have been used to seal wine bottles since early in the 17th century. Recently, consumers and winemakers have begun to rebel against the large number of wines that become "corked" (go bad due to a tainted cork). This, along with the accompanying cost savings, has sparked the increased usage of screw caps on fine wines and hence the debate.

Put a cork in it! Support for the cork:

> Romance – Screw caps degrade the tradition and wonderful ritual of opening a bottle of wine.
> Complexity – Secondary flavors develop as the wine ages
> Balanced Respiration – The cork can absorb some sulfides, thereby improving the character of the wine.

Screw this one! Support for the screw-cap:

> Price – Screw caps are much cheaper to buy and just as effective.
> Accessibility – Screw caps remove mystique from wine, making it more appealing to the masses.
> Consistent Taste – Wine retains original fruit aromas and flavors with age.

So, which one is best? I think the answer lies in a quote from Wolf Blass, "It all depends on whether you are a puller or a screwer!"

CRAIG'S MUSHROOM ALMOND PÂTÉ

This meatless pate is best prepared four to six days in advance. Use of a food processor is assumed in the directions but is not required.

Difficulty: ❡❡❡
Preparation Time: 40 minutes plus setting time
Yield: 6 servings

3 teaspoons butter
1 teaspoon fresh thyme (or 1 tablespoon fresh rosemary)
1 cup slivered almonds
1/2 cup fresh parsley
1/2 onion
1/2 pound mushrooms
1 clove garlic
1/2 teaspoon salt
1/2 teaspoon pepper
2 tablespoons dry Vermouth or Cognac

1. In a frying pan, melt one tablespoon butter over medium heat and sauté almonds until golden brown. Remove to a bowl and wipe out pan.(Almonds can also be toasted in an enamel pan without butter, if desired.)

2. Chop parsley until very fine in a food processor with the metal blade. Set aside. Chop onion. Heat two tablespoons butter in pan and sauté onions until soft and transparent. Chop garlic followed by the mushrooms with quick pulses (being careful not to over-process). Add garlic and mushrooms to onions in pan and sauté until liquid evaporates. Add thyme, salt, and pepper. Stir and remove from heat.

3. Reserve two tablespoons of almonds and process the rest until finely ground. Do not over-grind. Add mushroom mixture and vermouth, processing enough to blend. Add reserved almonds and all but two tablespoons of parsley. Pulse to incorporate. Press mixture into a crock or bowl and sprinkle with remaining parsley. Refrigerate several days to allow flavors to blend.

4. Serve with slices of crusty French bread and a sampling of flavored mustards.

Contributed by Oakstone Winery

EGGPLANT AND ZUCCHINI

Difficulty: ♟♟
Preparation Time: 1 hour
Yield: 10 servings

1 medium eggplant, chopped
6 medium zucchini, chopped
2 slices bacon
1 onion, chopped
1 clove garlic, minced
1/2 teaspoon salt
1/4 teaspoon pepper
1/4 cup Rosé or blush wine
1/3 cup dry bread crumbs
1/3 cup Parmesan cheese, grated
1/4 teaspoon paprika

1. Heat oven to 325°.

2. In a saucepan, boil eggplant and zucchini in salted water until tender crisp, approximately 10 minutes. Drain and set aside.

3. In a skillet, fry bacon until lightly browned. Add onion and garlic and sauté for 15 minutes.

4. Place bacon mixture, eggplant and zucchini in a buttered, 3-quart baking dish. Add all remaining ingredients and mix thoroughly. Bake for 40 minutes.

"May your heart be light and happy,
May your smile be big and wide,
And may your pockets always have
A coin or two inside!"
-Irish Toast

FIELD GREENS WITH SUSAN'S VINAIGRETTE

Difficulty: 🍷🍷

Preparation Time: 25 minutes plus 1 hour chilling time

Yield: 8 servings

8 cups mixed field greens
2 Roma tomatoes, diced
1 cup blueberries
Salt and cracked pepper, to taste
1/2 cup goat cheese
1/3 cup toasted, sliced almonds
1 cucumber, scraped lengthwise with a fork to leave ridges
  and thinly sliced

Susan's Vinaigrette:
1/2 cup Chenin Blanc
1 cup extra virgin olive oil
1 tablespoon balsamic vinegar
1/4 cup apple cider vinegar
1 teaspoon Worchestershire Sauce
1 tablespoon plus 2 teaspoons white granulated sugar
1 tablespoon brown sugar
1/2 teaspoon salt

1. For dressing, pour wine in small pan and boil until reduced by half.

2. Put reduced wine and remaining vinaigrette ingredients into a 2-cup jar. Cover tightly. Shake vigorously until well emulsified.

3. Coat cucumber with some dressing. Chill cucumber and remaining dressing for one hour.

4. Toss mixed field greens with diced tomatoes and blueberries in a bowl.

5. Lightly toss with vinaigrette. Add salt and pepper to taste.

6. Mound greens on serving plate. Sprinkle with cold goat cheese and toasted almonds. Garnish with cucumber slices and serve.

Contributed by Susan Auler of Fall Creek Vineyards

Nebuchadnezzar and Methuselah never had it so good! Have you ever noticed the super-sized bottles of wine or Champagne at restaurants and tasting rooms? Quite a few wineries will customize these attractive bottles for your company or special event. This is a fun way to make a lasting impression.

You may hear someone refer to the standard bottle as a "fifth." Now rounded off metrically to 750 ml, the bottle was originally one-fifth of a gallon. The half bottle or "tenth" was originally one-tenth of a gallon. For standardization purposes, the United States converted to metric sizing for wine bottles on January 1, 1979.

The chart below will help you get to know wine bottle names:

Name	Measure	Size Equivalent	Servings**
Split*	187 ml	quarter bottle	1
Half Bottle (Tenth)	375 ml	half bottle	2
Bottle (Fifth)	750 ml	standard bottle	5
Magnum	1.5 liters	2 bottles	10
Double Magnum	3 liters	4 bottles	20
Jeroboam*	3 liters	4 bottles	20
Rehoboam	4.5 liters	6 bottles	30
Imperial	6 liters	8 bottles	40
Methuselah*	6 liters	8 bottles	40
Salmanazar	9 liters	12 bottles	61
Balthazar	12 liters	16 bottles	81
Nebuchadnezzar	15 liters	20 bottles	101
Sovereign	50 liters	67 bottles	338

*Champagne bottle name. **Approximate 5 oz. servings.

FRESH CORN AND LOBSTER BISQUE

Difficulty: ♟♟♟
Preparation Time: 1 hour 15 minutes
Yield: 8 servings

4 tablespoons sweet butter
2 cups corn kernels, freshly cut off cob
2 cups onion, chopped
3 stalks celery, chopped
2 carrots, chopped
1 cup Natural Champagne
1 cup chopped tomato
10 cups lobster broth
1/4 cup basmati rice
1 cup cooked lobster meat
Kosher salt and pepper to taste
1/2 cup heavy cream
1/2 cup dry Sherry

1. In a soup pot, sauté onions, celery, carrots and corn in butter. Season with salt and pepper. Add Champagne and cook 5 minutes.

2. Add tomatoes and broth. Simmer for 30 minutes.

3. Add rice and cook another 20 minutes.

4. Add cream and bring to a boil. Add lobster and Sherry, then remove from heat. Purée in blender and serve immediately.

Contributed by Chef Robin Lehnhoff of Korbel Champagne Cellars

GREEN ASPARAGUS WITH OLIVE OIL SABAYON

Difficulty: ❡❡❡
Preparation Time: 35 minutes
Yield: 3 servings

1 cup dry white wine
2 egg yolks, lightly beaten
1/3 cup extra virgin olive oil
1 pound green asparagus, peeled
Salt and freshly ground white pepper

1. In a saucepan, bring white wine to just below the boiling point over medium-high heat. Continue cooking until liquid is reduced by three-quarters, then allow to cool and transfer to the top of a double boiler.

2. Whisk egg yolks into wine reduction. Set over simmering water over medium-high heat and cook, whisking constantly, until yolks thicken enough to fall into thin ribbons when whisk is lifted from pan. Remove top of double boiler from bottom and, off heat, gradually whisk in olive oil. Thin, if necessary, with 1-2 tablespoons water or white wine. Season to taste with salt and pepper and set aside.

3. Peel asparagus two-thirds up the stalk and tie in bundles of 12-18 with kitchen string. In a deep saucepan with water, bring to a boil over medium-high heat. Reduce heat to medium, and cook until asparagus is tender, about 10 minutes. Untie bundle, transfer to a platter, and spoon sauce over asparagus.

Contributed by Jordan Vineyard & Winery

HEIRLOOM TOMATO SOUP
Difficulty: ♟♟♟
Preparation Time: 35 minutes
Yield: 4 servings

2 tablespoons olive oil
1 yellow onion, roughly chopped
Salt and pepper, to taste
3 cloves garlic, minced
1 pinch red chili flakes
1/4 cup Zinfandel
4 cups chicken or vegetable stock
4 cups heirloom tomatoes, preferably Brandywine (use only one
  variety)
Mozzarella croutons (recipe follows)
4 medium basil leaves, chiffonade

1. Heat olive oil in stockpot. Add onions, season with salt and
pepper and cook until translucent. Stir in garlic and chili flakes, cook
2 minutes. De-glaze pan with wine, reduce by half, and add chicken
stock and tomatoes. Bring to boil. Once boiling, reduce to a simmer
and cook for 20 minutes.

2. With a hand held buerre mixer, blend soup until smooth, and pass
through a fine mesh strainer. Check for seasoning. When ready to
serve, ladle soup into bowls and top with two croutons and a
sprinkling of basil.

Mozzarella Croutons:
12 slices sourdough baguette
Olive oil, for brushing
2 large balls of fresh mozzarella (the lightly salted kind), sliced

1. Heat oven to 425°.

2. Brush one side of baguette slice with olive oil. Arrange slices on a
baking sheet, bake 10 to 15 minutes or until golden brown. Reduce
heat to 350°. Just before serving the soup, top croutons with a slice of
mozzarella and place in the oven until cheese is slightly softened,
approximately 2 minutes.

Contributed by Lambert Bridge Winery

wine wit

LAYERED PORTABELLA BURGERS

Difficulty: 🍷🍷

Preparation Time: 1 1/2 hours including marinating time
Yield: 4 burgers

1 garlic clove, crushed
1/4 cup olive oil
1 cup Cabernet Sauvignon
4 Portabella mushroom caps
1 small eggplant, peeled and sliced 1/4-inch thick
Olive oil
Garlic salt
4 seeded hamburger buns, split and toasted
4 lettuce leaves
4 tomato slices
4 Provolone cheese slices
Condiments of your choice (BBQ sauce is great.)
Nonstick spray

1. Mix first three ingredients together and pour into a large zip-lock bag. Add mushroom caps and marinate for 1 hour.

2. Heat oven to 350°. Grease cookie sheet with non-stick spray.

3. Place eggplant slices on cookie sheet. Brush each slice with olive oil and sprinkle with garlic salt. Bake for 15 minutes, then broil for 4-5 minutes until golden brown. Keep warm.

4. Grill or broil the marinated mushroom caps for a few minutes on each side.

5. To assemble your burgers, layer the bottom bun with lettuce, tomato, mushroom cap, cheese slice and eggplant slice. Top with all your favorite burger fixins'.

Contributed by Pleasant Hill Winery

LENTIL-APPLE SOUP

Difficulty: 🍷🍷
Preparation Time: 1 hour
Yield: 6 servings

2 tablespoons extra virgin olive oil
1 cup thinly sliced leeks
1 cup Fuji apple, seeded and diced
1 cup Sauvignon Blanc
1 cup apple juice
3 cups vegetable stock
1 cup dry lentils
2 bay leaves
1 1/2 cups Yukon gold potatoes, peeled, diced and resting in water
Kosher salt and ground black pepper, to taste
2 tablespoons fresh lemon juice
1 tablespoons fresh thyme leaves
1 tablespoons fresh chopped parsley

1. Sauté leeks and apples in olive oil until soft.

2. Add wine, apple juice and stock. Bring to a boil then add lentils and bay leaves. Cook for 30 minutes.

3. Add diced potatoes. Cook another 15 minutes. Season with salt, pepper and lemon juice.

4. Remove bay leaves and purée soup in blender until smooth.

5. Reheat, adding fresh thyme and parsley just before serving.

Contributed by Chef Robin Lenhoff of Kenwood Vineyards

MAYER'S HUNGARIAN GOULASH

Serve this hearty dish in soup bowls with crusty bread. All vegetables and amounts can be modified to taste.

Difficulty: ♟♟
Preparation Time: 2 hours
Yield: 8 servings

2 pounds beef or veal stew meat
Cooking oil
1 large onion, chopped
1 large carrot, chopped
2 or 3 potatoes, peeled and chopped
1/2 medium zucchini, chopped
1/2 green pepper, chopped
4 mushrooms, chopped
1/2 large tomato, chopped
2 ounces frozen peas
1 1/2 cups water
1/2 cup white wine or Champagne
3 tablespoons Hungarian paprika
Spices (to taste): garlic powder, onion powder, freshly ground black
  pepper, parsley flakes

1. Trim and cube meat.

2. Sauté onion in a Dutch oven. Add meat to pot and brown with onion, adding paprika over the meat.

3. Add vegetables (except peas), water, wine and spices

4. Cover and simmer for about 1 1/2 hours or until meat is tender, stirring occasionally and adding spices if needed

5. Add peas and simmer an additional 5 minutes.

WineWisdom

"Wine is a magician, for it loosens the tongue and liberates good stories."
~Homer~

"Come quickly, I am tasting stars!"
~Dom Perignon, upon first tasting Champagne~

"My only regret in life is that I did not drink more Champagne."
~John Maynard Keynes~

"Decanter: n. A vessel whose functions are most envied by the human stomach."
~Ambrose Bierce~

"Wine makes daily living easier, less hurried, with fewer tensions and more tolerance."
~Benjamin Franklin~

"As far as I am concerned there are only two types of wine, those I like and those I don't."
~André Launay~

"Old wine and an old friend are good provisions."
~George Herbert~

"A glass of wine is a great refreshment after a hard day's work."
~Ludwig von Beethoven~

"Let first the onion flourish there, rose among roots, the maiden fair wine-scented . . ."
~Robert Louis Stevenson~

"Wine is sunlight, held together by water."
~Galileo~

ONION SOUP GRATINÉE

Difficulty: ♟♟♟
Preparation Time: 1 hour
Yield: 8 servings

4 yellow onions, peeled and thinly sliced
1 tablespoon butter
1/2 cup red wine
1/2 cup white wine
1 quart vegetable stock
1 bay leaf
1 cup Idaho potatoes, diced to 1/2-inch
16 slices Swiss or Gruyére cheese
8 slices toasted country bread
Salt and pepper to taste

1. Melt butter in a large stock pot. Sauté onion slices until translucent. Add red wine and white wine, then reduce for 5 minutes.

2. Add vegetable stock, bay leaf, diced potatoes and salt and pepper. Simmer for 40 minutes.

3. Remove bay leaf and ladle into soup bowls. Place toasts on top of soup and cheese on top of bread. Place bowls under the broiler and brown until cheese is golden. Serve immediately. Bon appetit!

Contributed by Chef Didier Poirier of 71 Palm Restaurant

PARMESAN PARSLEY SPINACH SOUP

Difficulty: ♟♟
Preparation Time: 45 minutes
Yield: 6 servings

10-ounce package chopped frozen spinach
1/4 cup minced red onion
1 tablespoon extra virgin olive oil
1 tablespoon minced garlic
1/3 cup parsley, chopped
1 1/2 cups water
1/2 cup Merlot
2 teaspoons chicken bouillon
6 tablespoons sour cream
2 teaspoons honey
1/4 teaspoons sea salt
Zest from one small lime
Cracked pepper, to taste
Parmesan cheese, grated

1. Microwave spinach in box for 10 minutes on high.

2. In a skillet over medium heat, sauté red onion in olive oil until soft. Add garlic and parsley and continue cooking for a minute or two, being careful not to crisp the garlic.

3. Pour water and wine into a saucepan. Bring to a rolling boil, then boil for 1 minute. Turn off heat and add bouillon, stirring until dissolved.

4. Scrape contents of skillet into blender. Add spinach along with half of bouillon mixture. Blend well. Add remainder of liquid, sour cream, honey, salt, zest and pepper. Blend well.

5. Chill at least 15 minutes to cool and meld the flavors. Serve at room temperature in cup with grated Parmesan on top.

Contributed by Susan Auler of Fall Creek Vineyards

CORKBOARD

A raisin dropped into a glass of sparkling wine will repeatedly bounce up and down between the top and the bottom of the glass.

Here's a tip on how to prevent a sparkling wine from foaming out of the glass: Pour one ounce into the glass; this will settle quickly. Now pour the remainder of the serving into this starter and it will not foam as much.

The longest recorded Champagne cork flight was 177 feet and 9-inches, 4 feet from level ground at Woodbury Vineyards in New York State.

Early winemakers viewed bubbles in Champagne as a highly undesirable defect to be prevented.

Champagne is generally made from one of three grapes: Pinot Noir, Pinot Meunier and Chardonnay. The first two are black grapes and the latter is white.

At 90 pounds per square inch, the pressure in a bottle of Champagne is nearly triple the pressure in automobile tires.

If you see a bottle with the word "Champagne" on the label, as opposed to sparkling wine, it guarantees that the wine has been produced in the cold, northern French region of Champagne. Like all appellations, however, this does not ensure quality.

Residual sugar levels in Champagne that are listed on the labels are generally categorized as follows: BRUT (0-1.5 % residual sugar), EXTRA DRY (1.2-2.0 % residual sugar), SEC (1.7-3.5 % residual sugar), DEMI-SEC (3.3-5.0 % residual sugar), DOUX (5.0 + % residual sugar).

Brut is the most popular style of Champagne, and the best grapes are saved for this category.

PEAR, CHEDDAR CHEESE AND WALNUT SALAD WITH WARM PORT AND BALSAMIC VINEGAR DRESSING

This salad makes a great pre-entree appetizer for any dinner and was adapted from a recipe from the Walnut Marketing Board. If Tillamook extra sharp aged cheese is not available, any blue veined cheese such as Stilton, Gorgonzola or Oregon Blue could be substituted with good results.

Difficulty: ♟♟
Preparation Time: 20 minutes
Yield: 8 servings

3/4 pound fresh mixed salad greens
1/4 pound fresh spinach, destemmed
2 medium ripe pears
1 1/2 cup walnuts
2 cups Tillamook extra-sharp aged cheddar cheese, crumbled
1 cup Ruby Port
1 tablespoon brown sugar
1/4 cup balsamic vinegar
1/4 cup virgin olive oil
Fresh ground black pepper (optional)

1. Heat oven to 350°.

2. Spread walnuts on baking sheeting and toast in an oven until lightly browned. Coarsely chop and set aside.

3. Remove stems from washed spinach and tear into small pieces. Mix spinach with greens in bowl. Arrange mix in heaps on eight salad plates. Cut approximately 1/2-inch off top of pears, core and slice into 1/8-inch slices. Arrange 3 to 4 slices on top of greens on each plate and divide the cheese and walnuts among them.

4. Reduce the Port by half over medium-high heat in a small sauce pan. Stir in sugar and dissolve. Remove from heat, stir in balsamic vinegar and slowly whisk in olive oil.

5. While mixture is still warm, drizzle over each salad. Lightly season (optionally) with fresh ground pepper.

Contributed by Hinzerling Winery

SAUTÉED MUSHROOMS

Serve as a side dish, over grilled steaks, or on grilled burgers.

Difficulty: 🍷
Preparation Time: 25 minutes
Yield: 6 servings

2-3 pounds large mushrooms
1 small onion, finely chopped
1/2 cup butter (do not substitute)
4 tablespoons Worcestershire sauce
1 tablespoon soy sauce
1/2 cup dry red wine

1. Wash mushrooms and slice each from top to bottom into fairly thick pieces. Melt butter in a skillet and sauté onion and mushrooms for 5 minutes.

2. Add the Worcestershire, soy sauce and wine. Continue cooking until most of the moisture cooks away and the remaining liquid is thickening. Turn heat to very low. Cover and cook for 10 minutes more.

SHERRY SOUP

Difficulty: ▮
Preparation Time: 15 minutes
Yield: 6 servings

10 1/2-ounce can of green pea soup
10 1/2-ounce can of mushroom soup
10 1/2-ounce can of tomato soup
2 cups half and half
7-ounce can minced clams
1/3 cup Sherry
Parsley, chopped (optional)

1. Mix first 5 ingredients together and simmer for 10 minutes.

2. Add Sherry and mix well. Garnish with chopped parsley if desired.

JAZZ AND WINE

Two art forms that are intrinsically related are jazz and wine. One blends the music to please the ear and the other blends the grapes to please the palate. It is the perfect pairing that takes you to a place of relaxation and contentment.

Whether you are listening to Brian Culbertson, Noble Sissle, Acoustic Alchemy, Frankie Trumbauer, Chuck Mangione, Sade or Count Basie you can't go wrong. John Coltrane, Miles Davis, Kenny G, Fattburger, Spyro Gyra and others will take you to an unforgettable place as you enjoy a fine glass of wine.

Various wineries feature live jazz concerts in the vineyards. These concerts are often accompanied by wine tastings and gourmet meals. The cool, clear evening outdoors combined with the smooth jazz inevitably creates a night to remember. Wine and music festivals feature world-class performances from top jazz artists. Breathtaking views, wine tasting and sizzling jazz . . . you can't beat it. Explore the sensations and create special moments when you pair jazz and wine.

SIMA (STUFFING) FOR TURKEY

For small turkey. Recipe must be doubled for average-sized turkey.

Difficulty: ❢
Preparation Time: 25 minutes plus roasting time
Yield: 6 Servings

1 onion, chopped
4 tablespoons olive oil
2 tablespoons butter (can substitute olive oil)
2 cloves garlic, pressed
2 packages frozen chopped spinach, drained
1/2 cup chopped parsley
5 eggs (or 7 egg whites)
2 cups bread crumbs
1/4 cup grated Parmesan cheese
Dash of basil, salt and pepper
1 cup white wine

1. Sauté onion and garlic in oil and butter.

2. In large bowl, add onion mixture to remaining ingredients and mix well.

3. Stuff turkey and bake as directed or bake separately, covered, in oven at 350° until firm.

Contributed by Stevenot Winery

Send in the clones! Grapevines do not reproduce reliably from seed. To cultivate a particular grape variety with the best character possible, grafting (a plant version of cloning) is used. Clonal selection began in Germany in 1926 and is now used in most grape growing countries. Cuttings are taken from a single vine called the mother vine. All vines grown from the mother vine and future generations will be identical. The right clonal selection complements the terrior and gives winemakers the best possible material for their wines.

SPICY ZINFANDEL STEW

Difficulty: ♟♟♟

Preparation Time: 2 hours

Yield: 8 servings

1 34-ounce can plum tomatoes
1 cup frozen "petite" corn kernels
2 pounds beef chuck
6 cloves garlic (to taste)
2 large yellow onions
1/2 green bell pepper
5 small to medium potatoes
1 1/2 tablespoons olive oil
4 tablespoons Worcestershire sauce
Salt, to taste
1 tablespoon cumin
1 tablespoon paprika
1/2 teaspoon chili powder
1 teaspoon oregano
1/2 cup fresh rosemary
1 3/4 cup Zinfandel
2 cups beef stock
Flour to thicken, if desired

1. Drain tomatoes. Cut the beef into 1-inch or smaller cubes and sprinkle with salt. Cut potatoes into small cubes. Mince the garlic, onions, pepper, and rosemary.

2. In a large, deep pan, heat oil. Add the onion and cook until soft, about 3 minutes. Add the garlic and green pepper and cook until golden. Remove from pan and set aside.

3. Add Worcestershire sauce to pan, add beef and sear over medium-high heat until browned. Stir in spices and herbs and cook for 30 minutes.

4. Add the Zinfandel and stir with a wooden spoon to de-glaze the bottom of the pan. Add the onion mixture, tomatoes, and beef stock. Reduce heat, cover and simmer until meat is tender, about 1 2/3 hours.

5. Add corn and heat through. Thicken with flour stirred into beef broth or water, if stew is too thin. Can be made up to two days ahead.

Contributed by Mill Creek Vineyards

SWEETLY SPICED ZUCCHINI

Difficulty: 🍷
Preparation Time: 20 minutes
Yield: 4 servings

1 medium onion, finely chopped
1 garlic clove, minced
1/3 cup parsley, chopped
2 tablespoons butter
1 pound zucchini, sliced 1/4-inch thick
8-ounce can tomato sauce
1/3 cup dry white wine
1 tablespoon sugar
1/2 teaspoon nutmeg
1/2 teaspoon salt
1/2 teaspoon cinnamon
1/4 teaspoon pepper
1/2 cup Parmesan cheese, grated

1. Heat butter in skillet and sauté onion, garlic and parsley for 6 minutes. Add zucchini slices. Cover and simmer on low for another 6 minutes.

2. Stir in tomato sauce, wine, sugar, nutmeg, salt, cinnamon and pepper. Cover and simmer again for 5 minutes, stirring frequently.

3. Just before serving, stir in the cheese.

VENISON STUFFED CABERNET MUSHROOMS

"Whenever we introduce a new vintage, we like to do it with a food pairing. Our Cabernet Sauvignon from the Texas Davis Mountains was perfectly paired with venison stuffed mushrooms. The hard part is putting the recipe down on paper. Sicilians cook as a family/social gathering – a little of this, a pinch of that. I grew up with traditional Sicilian cuisine and not one recipe is on paper! Keep that in mind as you make these stuffed mushrooms. I'll work on getting the family recipes written down." -Chef Jeanne Cottle

Difficulty: 🍷🍷
Preparation Time: 30 minutes
Yield: 12 servings

1 pound lean venison sausage, cooked
Approximately 1/2 cup Italian seasoned bread crumbs
1 pound large white mushrooms
Approximately 11/2 cups Cabernet Sauvignon
Minced garlic
Salt
Pepper

1. Heat oven to 300°.

2. Clean and destem mushrooms.

3. Mix venison with bread crumbs. Moisten with some Cabernet. Mix well. Stuff the mushroom caps with the mixture and put in a single layer in a glass baking pan.

4. In a saucepan, cook down the remaining Cabernet. Add minced garlic, salt and pepper to taste. Pour the sauce over the mushrooms. Bake for 15 minutes and enjoy with a glass of Cabernet Sauvignon.

Contributed by Chef Jeanne Cottle of Pleasant Hill Winery

WINE-MARINATED GREEN BEANS

This marinade also works well with artichoke hearts, snap peas or pole beans.

Difficulty: 🍷🍷

Preparation Time: 15 minutes plus standing time

Yield: 4-6 servings

11/2 pounds fresh or frozen green beans, cooked
1 cup salad oil
1/2 cup white wine vinegar
1/2 cup dry white wine
1/4 cup red onion, chopped
1 tablespoon parley, chopped
1 teaspoon garlic, finely chopped
1/2 teaspoon salt
1/2 teaspoon seasoned pepper

1. Cool cooked green beans and place in a dish.

2. Combine all other ingredients and mix well.

3. Pour over green beans and let stand for at least 3 hours before serving to allow flavors to blend.

"One bottle for four of us;
Thank God there's no more of us!"
– Irish Toast

ZUCCHINI SOUP WITH PARMESAN CROUTONS

Difficulty: 🍴🍴

Preparation Time: 30 minutes

Yield: 8 servings

3 tablespoons butter
1 tablespoon olive oil
2 yellow onions, cut in half and sliced
2 cloves garlic, minced
3 pounds zucchini, remove ends and slice
1 cup Sauvignon Blanc
Salt and pepper, to taste
3 cups chicken or veggie stock, or water
1/2 cup heavy whipping cream
1/4 teaspoon nutmeg, finely grated

1. In a large stockpot, heat butter and olive oil together. Add onions and cook until transparent.

2. Add garlic and zucchini, stir and cook for 5 minutes. De-glaze the pan with wine and add salt and pepper.

3. Once wine has reduced by half, add stock and season. Bring to a boil and cook until zucchini is soft enough to purée.

4. In a blender, Cuisinart or with a hand held buerre mixer, purée soup to desired consistency. Stir in cream and nutmeg, check for seasonings.

5. Ladle into bowls and top with croutons.

Parmesan & Oregano Croutons:

11/2 cups day old French bread, cut into small cubes
1/4 cup olive oil
2 tablespoons fresh oregano, finely chopped
1/4 cup grated Parmesan cheese
Salt, to taste

1. Heat oven to 375°.

2. Toss cubed bread with olive oil. Bake until the croutons are a light golden brown. As soon as the croutons are removed from the oven, toss with oregano, cheese and a little salt. Let cool.

Contributed by Lambert Bridge Winery

WINEWISDOM

"The wine had such ill-effects on Noah's health, that it was all he could do to live 950 years."
 ~Will Rogers~

"When I take wine, my cares go to rest."
 ~Anacreon~

"Wine rouses the heart, inclines to passion."
 ~Ovid~

"I am not old but mellow like good wine."
 ~Stephen Phillips~

"Wine, madam, is God's next best gift to man."
 ~Ambrose Bierce~

"Polished brass is the mirror of the body and wine of the heart."
 ~Aeschylus~

"Those lodes and pockets of earth, more precious than the precious ores … And the wine is bottled poetry."
 ~Robert Louis Stevenson~

"Drink a glass of wine after your soup, and you steal a ruble from the doctor."
 ~Russian Proverb~

"Only those in the midst of it can one fully comprehend the joys of wine . . ."
 ~Li Po~

"I know of no other liquid that, placed in the mouth, forces one to think."
 ~Clifton Fadiman~

$\mathcal{S}$HAPE DOES MATTER

The shape of the wine glass can impact your enjoyment of a nice wine. In the 1950's, Claus Josef Riedel discovered that matching the shape and volume of the wine glass to the wine could actually make it taste better.

His research showed that a glass with a larger and broader bowl worked best for the bold red wines with bigger bouquets, while a tulip-shaped glass with a narrower bowl worked well for the more delicate aromas of most white wines.

Dessert wines should be served in a smaller glass with a narrower opening to concentrate the rich aromas of these wines. Champagne is to be served in glasses, called flutes, that are narrow with a narrow opening. The smaller opening leaves less surface area for the bubbles to escape.

Below are several wine glasses? Can you identify which shape is most appropriate for each type of wine?

a.   b.   c.   d.

Most experts will recommend that you select glasses made of crystal or other thin clear glass, that is not decorative or colored. The clear glass allows you to more easily view and appreciate the color, legs and tears of the wine you are drinking.

Finally, hand wash your glasses with hot water and then dry immediately with a towel to avoid streaks and smears.

Solutions:
a. Red Wine   b. White Wine   c. Champagne   d. Dessert Wine

FRUITS

AVOCADOS STUFFED WITH CRABMEAT

Difficulty: ♟♟♟

Preparation Time: 1 hour

Yield: 4 main dish or 8 side dish servings

4 ripe avocados
4 cloves garlic, minced
6 cups sauce (recipe below)
2 pounds crabmeat, well drained
1/2 cup celery, chopped
1/2 cup green onion, chopped
5 egg whites, stiffly beaten
Fresh Parmesan cheese
Grated bread crumbs
1/4 cup melted butter
Juice of 2 lemons

Sauce:
4 tablespoons butter
4 tablespoons flour
1 1/2 teaspoons salt
Dash cayenne, to taste
4 cups half and half
8 egg yolks, well beaten
1/2 cup Sherry

1. Heat oven to 350°.

2. To prepare avocados: Cut avocado in half lengthwise and discard the seed. Score the inside and add minced garlic and lemon juice. Let stand for 1/2 hour at room temperature, then discard garlic and juice.

Sauce:
Melt butter, stir in flour, salt and cayenne until very well blended. Add half and half and cook over low heat, stirring constantly. Bring sauce to a boil. Remove from heat. Place egg yolks in a large mixing bowl and stir sauce into the egg yolks a little at a time until well blended and smooth. Stir in Sherry. Set aside.

Crabmeat stuffing:

Mix drained crabmeat, celery, green onion and sauce. (Note: add the sauce gradually as to not make the stuffing too runny. You may not need all six cups). Fold in egg whites. Fill avocados with crabmeat mixture. Sprinkle with bread crumbs and Parmesan cheese. Drizzle melted butter on top and bake for 25 minutes.

Contributed by Oakstone Winery

How does one know when to harvest wine grapes? Samples are selected from clusters in the vineyard and the testing begins. The brix scaling system is used to measure the sugar levels in grapes. Three methods for testing sugar levels include the refractometer, hydrometer and taste.

A refractometer is a small telescope-looking gadget that is used to gauge sugar level by measuring density using light influenced by temperature. A hydrometer is a glass tube with a weighted end that measures juice density. It is placed in a beaker filled with grape juice. Adjusted for temperature, the density of the juice determines the amount of sugar present. In addition to scientific methods, tasting is still a key determinant for knowing when to harvest grapes. Does the fruit taste ripe?

CORKBOARD

RUDY

Among the world's fruit crops, wine grapes rank #1 in the number of acres planted.

American wine drinkers consume more wine on Thanksgiving than any other day of the year.

The number of wineries in the U.S. has tripled in the last 20 years.

More than 85% of U.S. wine consumption is accomplished by less than 8% of the total population.

Ninety-five percent of all the wine made each year is consumed before the next harvest.

Roughly 10,000 varieties of wine grapes exist worldwide.

It takes about 4 to 5 years to harvest a commercial crop from newly planted grape vines.

Alcohol consumption decreases during the time of the full moon.

White wine gets darker as it ages while red wine gets lighter.

"The quick brown fox jumps over the lazy dog" is often thought to be the only English sentence to include all the letters of the alphabet. Here's another one: "Pack my box with five dozen liquor jugs."

A bota is a goatskin bag for holding wine.

In the 1600s, thermometers were filled with brandy instead of mercury.

Letters from "drink to your health" can be used to spell "ideal heart diet." Drinking alcohol in moderation can significantly reduce the risk of heart disease.

BLACKBERRY-CABERNET CHOCOLATE TRUFFLES

Difficulty: ❢❢❢
Preparation Time: 45 minutes plus chilling time
Yield: 4 dozen

1 pound Callebaut bittersweet chocolate
1 cup heavy cream
1 pint fresh or frozen blackberries
1/2 cup blackberry Monin Syrup
1/2 cup Cabernet Sauvignon
1/2 cup Valrhona cocoa powder

1. Chop chocolate into small pieces for melting.

2. Scald cream in a saucepan. Stir in chocolate. Turn off heat and continue to stir until chocolate is melted.

3. In another pan, combine berries, syrup and wine. Cook until liquid is reduced by half.

4. Purée berry mixture in blender and pour through strainer into chocolate mixture. Fold until mixed well. Pour into pan and refrigerate until set.

5. Roll into 1/2-ounce balls. Dust with cocoa and store in a cool, dry place until ready to serve.

Contributed by Chef Robin Lehnhoff of Valley of the Moon Winery

PAIRING WINE WITH CHOCOLATE

The right wine with the right chocolate can offer an unparalleled taste treat! To complement each other, the wine should be as sweet or sweeter than the chocolate it is being served with. A bad match can cause the chocolate's sweetness to draw the fruit out of the wine and leave you with a case of dry mouth. To avoid a negative experience, a couple of pairings are recommended below:

White chocolate: Sherry or Orange Muscat
Milk chocolate: dessert wine, lighter Merlot, Muscat, Pinot Noir or
	Reisling
Dark (bittersweet) chocolate: Cabernet, Cabernet Sauvignon or
	Zinfandel

Wine Words

Part One *"Tasting", Continued from Page 34*

Earthy – This term refers to the flavors and smells that are derived from the soil where the grapes have been grown. A little is appealing, too much can make a wine "coarse".

Finish – This refers to the impression that a wine leaves in your mouth after it is swallowed: not only the flavors, but how long the taste lingers.

Firm – This relates to the aftertaste and refers to the taste at the very back of your palate which is caused by the tannins.

Flat – Describing a wine that is dull, boring or lifeless.

Fruity or Fruit Forward – Often used to denote a wine whose fruit flavors and aromas are noticeable. This term is most often used when talking about whites or lower tannin reds.

Green – This term is used often for young wines that have too much acidity.

Hard – Simply put, too much tannin!

Heavy – Meaning a wine with too much alcohol and acidity for the fruit and sugar levels.

Hot – Simply put, too much alcohol!

Jammy – A wine having a great intensity of fruit which contributes to a very flavorful, concentrated taste.

Lean – This denotes a wine lacking in fruit but not acidity.

Legs – When you swirl your glass of wine and watch the columns of wine that trickle down the glass, these are called its legs.

Continued on Page 110

CHAMPAGNE MELON SOUP

Difficulty: ♟♟

Preparation Time: 20 minutes plus chilling time
Yield: 6-8 servings

3 cups cantaloupe
3 cups honeydew
1 cup fresh orange juice
2 tablespoons fresh lime juice
1 1/2 tablespoons honey
2 cups Brut Champagne
Fresh mint leaves for garnish
Sugar

1. Purée cantaloupe, honeydew, orange juice, lime juice and honey in batches in a blender until very smooth.

2. Within a half hour of serving, add cold Champagne to soup. Stir to blend well.

3. Serve in chilled glasses rimmed with sugar. Garnish with mint leaves.

Contributed by Thornton Winery

"May neighbors respect you,
Trouble neglect you,
The angels protect you,
And heaven accept you."
– Irish Toast

BUZZ ON THE VINE

D on't be Afraid to Flambé!

Flambé is a French word that means "flaming". To flambé means to ignite a dish that has liquor added. This technique is often employed tableside at expensive restaurants for a dramatic effect. It allows you to add the flavor of liquor without the alcohol.

Impress your friends and family when you flambé a variety of foods at home. Several recipes in this book are enhanced by it. To flambé, choose a brandy or 80-proof liquor (40% alcohol) that is complementary to the food being cooked. Beer, Champagne and table wines will not work since they don't have a high enough level of alcohol. Liquors 120-proof and above are highly flammable and considered too dangerous for this use. Exercise caution as you flambé, since you will be dealing with a liquid that is on fire!

First, A Few Safety Warnings:
1. Only ignite the liquor with a long match. Light the edge of the pan and not the liquid itself and never lean over the pan while lighting.
2. Do not pour liquor directly from the bottle into a pan over an open flame. The flame could travel up to the bottle and cause an explosion.
3. Never carry a flaming dish. The flame could splash out of the pan causing a burn or starting a fire.
4. When you flambé for others to see, be careful not to ignite the liquor

near your guests or anything flammable. Set pan on an open, flat surface that is a safe distance away before igniting.

Your Flambé Masterpiece:
1. Use a flambé pan with rounded, deep sides and a long handle for the dish you are preparing.
2. Heat brandy or liquor over low flame in a tall saucepan until bubbles start to form around edges. You can also warm liquor in the microwave by heating in a microwave-safe dish for 30 seconds on high. Alcohol will boil at 175°F. If you allow it to boil, the alcohol will burn off and it will not flame.
3. When your menu item is ready and the liquor is warm, remove pan from heat and add alcohol. Ignite liquor immediately to avoid having the raw alcohol absorbed by the food. Let it burn until the flame disappears. At this point all the alcohol will have burned off. If you enjoy the alcohol flavoring, you can add more wine to the food once the flame has gone out. If you want flames without the alcohol in your food, simply soak sugar cubes in the alcohol. Place around the edge of the dish and light.
4. Serve immediately.

As long as you heed the warnings and follow the steps above, it is simple and fun to flambé. We suggest you use whiskey or cognac with meats and fruit-flavored brandies with fruits and desserts. So assemble your friends and family, dim the lights a bit, and ignite your flambé!

"Grow old with me!
The best is yet to be,
The last of life,
for which, the first is made."
– Robert Browning

CHILLED CANTALOUPE AND RASPBERRY SOUP

Difficulty: 🍷🍷
Preparation Time: 2 hours
Yield: 4 cups

1 large ripe cantaloupe, peeled, scooped and chopped
1 1/2 cups granulated sugar (varies with the sweetness of the melon)
3 cups fresh raspberries, pureed and strained, pips removed
3/4 cup plain yogurt
3/4 cup sour cream
2 cups sweet red or port wine
4 teaspoons fresh mint leaves, washed, for garnish
1 cup fresh raspberries, for garnish

1. Puree the cantaloupe and sugar in small batches in a food processor until smooth and sugar dissolves.

2. Transfer to bowl, whisk in yogurt, sour cream, raspberry puree and wine. Chill for 2 hours minimum, covered in the refrigerator.

3. Chill serving bowls. This can be garnished with additional yogurt or sour cream, whole fresh mint leaves and fresh raspberries.

Contributed by Chef Paul Mach courtesy of "You're the Chef" and Hunt Country Vineyards

The *Aroma Wheel* is a circular table that is used to describe wine in uniform, non-judgmental terms. Why? Aromas can be difficult to communicate. Years ago, oenologists at University of California at Davis interviewed wine lovers and wine tasters to generate a list of descriptive terms for the smells of wine. They ended up with a list of 12 major categories of wine smells, subdivided into 29 subcategories and 94 specific terms. The Aroma Wheel, available as a free download, allows you to develop your nose and vocabulary while you enjoy sipping wine.

WineWisdom

"It is not the year, the producer or even the label that determines the quality of the wine; it is the wine in the glass, whatever the label or producer or year . . . Drink wine, not labels."
~Maynard A. Amerine~

"Now and then it is a joy to have one's table red with wine and roses."
~Oscar Wilde~

"Good wine is a necessity of life for me."
~Thomas Jefferson~

". . . the best utilization of solar energy that we have found . . . Wine really is bottled sunshine."
~Emile Peynaud~

"May your love be good like wine, and grow stronger as it grows older."
~Old English Toast~

"Fill the bowl with flowing wine, and while your lips are wet press their fragrance into mine . . ."
~Anonymous~

"I love everything that's old: old friends, old times, old manners, old books, old wines."
~Oliver Goldsmith~

"A bottle of good wine, like a good act, shines ever in the retrospect."
~Robert Louis Stevenson~

"If a man deliberately abstains from wine to such an extent that he does serious harm to his nature, he will not be free from blame."
~Saint Thomas Aquinas~

"Language is wine upon the lips."
~Virginia Woolf~

CURRIED BANANAS

Difficulty: ♟♟
Preparation Time: 30 minutes
Yield: 6 servings

1/2 cup orange juice, without pulp
1/2 cup Riesling
1/2 cup firmly packed brown sugar
3 tablespoons butter, melted
2 tablespoons lemon juice
1/4 teaspoon curry powder
6 green-tipped bananas, peeled and cut in half lengthwise
Ice cream (optional)

1. Heat oven to 350°. Butter a 9x13-inch baking dish.

2. In a saucepan, combine orange juice, wine, brown sugar, butter, lemon juice and curry powder. Simmer until ingredients form a syrup.

3. Place bananas into baking dish in a single layer. Pour the sauce over the bananas and bake, uncovered, for 20 minutes, basting frequently.

4. Serve alone or à la mode.

DRUNKEN PEACHES AND BERRIES

Difficulty: 🍷🍷
Preparation Time: 20 minutes plus chilling time
Servings: 8

1 bottle (750 ml) Pinot Grigio or other dry white wine
1/2 cup sugar
1 orange
1 teaspoon cinnamon
6 peaches
1 pound raspberries or blackberries
Mint sprigs (optional)
16 Dutch Windmill cookies (optional)

1. Remove 1-inch x 2-inch strips of orange peel from orange (just orange part).

2. In a small saucepan, combine 1 cup wine, sugar, orange peel and cinnamon. Stir over low heat until sugar dissolves. Increase heat slightly and allow to simmer for 15 minutes. Remove from heat and add remaining wine.

3. Remove skin from peaches and cut lengthwise into slices. Place slices in large bowl. Wash raspberries and add to bowl. If you use frozen peach slices or berries, allow to thaw before adding to recipe.

4. Add wine mixture to berries. Cover and refrigerate for at least 2 hours.

5. Divide fruit and wine among chilled wine goblets. Garnish with mint sprigs. Serve with Dutch Windmill cookies or other wafer.

CELLAR CHALLENGE

Do you know your red wine grapes?

1. Syrah is a noble black grape variety that is thick-skinned and can grow almost anywhere. It is known as Syrah everywhere in the world except Australia. What do they call this grape in Australia?
    a.) Pinotage
    b.) Freisa
    c.) Baco Noir
    d.) Shiraz

2. This black-skinned French grape is believed to be a parent of the Cabernet Sauvignon grape.
    a.) Teroldego
    b.) Lagrein
    c.) Cabernet Franc
    d.) Grignolino

3. An exotic black grape that was brought to California in the 1800s, it is now seen as California's response to the French Claret.
    a.) Barbera
    b.) Zinfandel
    c.) Gamay
    d.) Grenache

4. In the 1990s this became the red varietal of choice. However, the movie *Sideways* (2004) dampened its sales as Miles Raymond was highly critical of it. "No, if anyone orders _____, I'm leaving. I am NOT drinking any (expletive) _____!"
    a.) Pinor Noir
    b.) Cabernet Sauvignon
    c.) Merlot
    d.) Grenache

 Solutions on page 241

76

FIG AND GOAT CHEESE CROSTINI

Difficulty: 🍷🍷
Preparation Time: 35 minutes
Yield: 24 pieces

3 tablespoons minced shallot
2 (3-inch) fresh thyme sprigs
1/4 California bay leaf
1 1/2 tablespoons unsalted butter
1/4 pound dried Black Mission figs, finely chopped
3/4 cup Port
1/4 teaspoon salt
1/8 teaspoon black pepper
1/2 teaspoon minced fresh thyme
12 (1/2-inch-thick) diagonally cut baguette slices
1 tablespoon olive oil
6 ounces soft mild goat cheese at room temperature
2 fresh ripe figs, cut into 1/2-inch pieces
Fresh thyme leaves, for garnish

1. Cook shallot, thyme sprigs, and bay leaf in butter in a medium heavy saucepan over moderately low heat, stirring, until shallot is softened, about 2 minutes.

2. Add dried figs, Port, salt and pepper and bring to a boil. Simmer, covered, until figs are soft, about 10 minutes. If there is still liquid in saucepan, remove lid and simmer, stirring, until most of liquid is evaporated, 3 to 4 minutes more.

3. Discard bay leaf and thyme sprigs and transfer jam to a bowl. Cool, then stir in minced thyme and salt and pepper to taste. Can be made up to 1 day ahead and chilled, uncovered. Bring to room temperature before assembling crostini.

Crostini:
1. Preheat oven to 350°.

2. Halve each baguette, slice diagonally, then arrange on a baking sheet and brush tops lightly with oil.

3. Bake on middle rack until lightly toasted, about 7 minutes.

4. Cool on baking sheet on a rack. Spread each toast with 1 teaspoon fig jam and top with about 1 1/2 teaspoons goat cheese and 2 pieces fresh fig.

Contributed by Gnekow Family Winery

FRUITY SLOW-COOKER HAM

Difficulty: ♟

Preparation Time: 7 hours and 15 minutes

Yield: 4 servings

2 ham slices, approximately 3/4- inch thick
1 cup cider
1 cup Port
1/2 cup maple syrup
3/4 cup cranberries
3/4 cup seedless grapes or raisins
4 whole cloves
Juice of one orange
6 slices of pineapple (optional)
2 tablespoons cornstarch
3 tablespoons water

1. Place ham slices in a slow-cooker, rolling slices to fit if necessary. Add remaining ingredients except cornstarch and water. Cover and cook on high for 1 hour, then on low for 6 hours.

2. Remove ham slices. To thicken sauce, set cooker on high. Mix cornstarch and water in small bowl. Stir mixture into slow-cooker and cook until thickened. Serve sauce over ham slices.

GRAVENSTEIN APPLE SOUP

Gravenstein Apples are one of Sonoma County's biggest crops behind grapes. This soup will take you back to a time when days were slow and life was simple.

Difficulty: ♟♟
Preparation Time: 50 minutes
Yield: 8 servings

3 tablespoons olive oil
1 bulb fresh fennel, diced
2 carrots, peeled and diced
2 stalks celery, diced
1 green bell pepper, diced
2 fresh tomatoes, diced
2 cups Chardonnay
3 cups chicken stock
6 apples, peeled, seeded and diced
3 tablespoons flour
1 tablespoon granulated sugar
3/4 cup heavy cream
2-3 tablespoons fresh lemon juice
Salt and pepper, to taste

1. Heat oil and cook fennel, carrots, celery, bell pepper and tomatoes for 5 minutes.

2. Add Chardonnay and let simmer for 5 minutes.

3. Add chicken stock and cook another 15 minutes.

4. Add apples to the pot and cook another 15 minutes.

5. In a separate bowl, make a slurry by whisking the flour and sugar into the cream. Stir into the soup and bring to a boil. Season with salt and pepper. Add lemon juice to lift the flavor.

Contributed by Chef Robin Lehnhoff of Lake Sonoma Winery

PORT-POACHED PEARS WITH BLUE CHEESE

Difficulty: ❗❗❗❗

Preparation Time: 1 1/2 hours plus chilling time

Yield: 6 servings

4 cups water
2 tablespoons fresh lemon juice
6 small ripe, but firm pears
2 1/2 cups Ruby Port
1 cinnamon stick
1/4 teaspoon whole peppercorns
1/2 cup blue veined cheese (Blue, Gorgonzola, Stilton, or Roquefort
  will work)
1/2 cup light cream cheese, softened

1. Combine juice and water in a large bowl. Peel each pear and remove core from bottom end. Leave stem on. Slice about 1/4-inch from bottom end so pear will sit upright, and place in water mixture.

2. Combine Ruby Port, peppercorns and cinnamon in a Dutch oven and bring to a boil. Reduce heat and simmer uncovered for about 5 minutes. Add pears and water, cover and simmer for 20 minutes or until pears are tender, turning fruit occasionally.

3. Remove pears with a slotted spoon and place in shallow dish. Bring cooking liquid to a boil, cook for 30 minutes or until reduced to about 3/4 cup. Strain and reserve liquid. Pour liquid over pears and chill for 8 hours turning fruit once or twice. Remove pears, reserve liquid and set aside.

4. Blend cheese in a food processor until smooth and creamy. Spoon into decorating bag with a small tube. Cut pears lengthwise into three or four wedges and arrange on top of sauce. Pipe some of the cheese blend onto the pears.

5. Serve with a small glass of Ruby Port!

Contributed by Hinzerling Winery

SASSY SUMMER SALAD

Difficulty: ❢
Preparation Time: 30 minutes
Yield: 4 servings

2 cups of mixed seasonal fruit, such as apples, plums, nectarines,
  peaches, blueberries, raspberries, blackberries, oranges, grapes, or
  bananas
Fresh lemon juice
Bottle of Orange Muscat wine

1. Cut fruit into bite-size chunks, saving apples and bananas for last to
prevent browning. Toss gently in a serving bowl.

2. Add lemon juice and wine to taste. Toss gently. Serve immediately
for a crisper salad or marinate for a juicier salad.

Contributed by Ventana Vineyards and Winery

"The last time that I trusted a dame was in Paris in 1940.
She was going out to get a bottle of wine. Two hours later, the
Germans marched into France."
~Sam Diamond in *Murder by Death* (1976)

"Oh, we could give it a try. I'll bring the wine, you bring your
scarred psyche."
~Chase in *Batman Forever* (1995)

"During one of my treks through Afghanistan, we lost our
corkscrew. We were compelled to live on food and water for
several days."
~Cuthbert J. Twillie in *My Little Chickadee* (1940)

"I know I don't have his looks. I know I don't have his money. I
know I don't have his connections, his knowledge of fine wines.
I know sometimes when I eat I get this clicking sound in my
jaw . . ."
  ~Wayne Campbell in *Wayne's World* (1992)

ELLAR HALLENGE

Did You Know?

1. It is the most widely-planted white wine grape in Italy. In France, it is known as Ugni Blanc. This grape is commonly used in Brandy and white Chianti. Do you know the Italian name for this grape?
   (a) Trebiano
   (b) Pinot Grigio
   (c) Fiano
   (d) Malvasia

2. In the 1860's, this state produced more wine than New York and California combined. Do you know the state?
   (a) Iowa
   (b) Indiana
   (c) Kentucky
   (d) Missouri

3. This fungus slowly rots grapes while they are ripening. This causes the water inside the grape to evaporate, leaving a sweet, more concentrated juice. The fungus is named:
   (a) Gray rot
   (b) Noble rot
   (c) Kombuca
   (d) Black rot

4. Written records of this Italian red grape date back as far as the late 1300s.
   (a) Aglianico
   (b) Refosco
   (c) Carignon
   (d) Baga

Solutions on page 241

SPICED CRANBERRY SAUCE WITH ZINFANDEL

Difficulty: 🍷
Preparation Time: 20 minutes plus cooling time
Yield: 6 servings

1 3/4 cup Zinfandel
1 cup sugar
1 cup packed golden brown sugar
6 whole cloves
6 whole allspice
2 cinnamon sticks
One 3x1-inch strip of orange peel
12 ounces fresh cranberries

1. Combine all ingredients except cranberries in a medium saucepan. Bring to a boil over medium heat, stirring until sugar dissolves. Reduce heat and simmer until reduced to 13/4 cups, about 10 minutes.

2. Strain syrup into a large saucepan. Add cranberries to syrup and cook over medium heat until berries burst, about 6 minutes. Cool. Transfer sauce to a bowl, cover and refrigerate until cold.

Contributed by Perry Creek Winery

*"May you have all the happiness
and luck that life can hold –
And at the end of all your rainbows,
May you find a pot of gold."
– Irish Toast*

SPICY WINE FRUIT

Difficulty: 🍷🍷
Preparation Time: 30 minutes plus chilling time
Yield: 6 servings

1 cinnamon stick
1/2 cup water
1/4 cup sugar
11 ounces mixed dried fruit
6 whole cloves
1/4 cup sweet red wine
2 tablespoons lemon juice
2 bananas

1. Tie cinnamon stick and cloves in cheesecloth bag. Bring cheesecloth bag, water, wine, sugar and lemon juice to boil in 2-quart saucepan.

2. Stir in dried fruit. Heat to boiling. Reduce heat and simmer uncovered for 10-15 minutes, stirring occasionally until fruit is plump and tender.

3. Refrigerate uncovered, stirring occasionally at least 3 hours but no longer than 24 hours.

4. Remove cheesecloth bag. Slice bananas and stir into fruit mixture until coated with syrup.

5. Drain fruit, reserving syrup. Serve fruit with some of the reserved syrup.

Try creating your own wine. There are many books and online sites dedicated to winemaking. Some wineries will provide the grapes and staff to help you blend your own special wine. A bit pricey, but an unforgettable experience. Too much work? Visit local wineries and take their winemaking tours. Tours and other special winemaker events can be informative and a lot of fun. They tend to give one a greater appreciation and love for wine.

Entertaining With an International Flair

Picking the international wines to cook with and serve is as much fun as planning the menu, table decorations and music. Although most countries offer fine selections of many varietals, here are some suggestions for selecting great wines from a few of the powerhouse wine-producing countries.

Spain – A Running of the Bulls Party

Ranking third in the world in wine production, Spain offers many unique and remarkable wine regions. In the last few decades, the renaissance in Spanish winemaking has excited wine drinkers worldwide.

Best bets for pairing with your Spanish fare:

Rioja – This rich red is the most common wine used to make the popular wine and fruit punch Sangria *(recipe page 236)*.
Tempranillo – Considered to be the grape behind Spain's finest wines, this wine can be compared to Pinot Noir and Cabernet Sauvignon.

Menu Suggestions:

Tapas – This Spanish cuisine of finger foods makes for a fun introduction to culinary tradition for your party. These aren't just appetizers, but a meal in Spain, where Tapas Bars are extremely popular and serve Tapas and Spanish wines. Tapas range the gamut from hot or cold, spicy or mild, meat and seafood based, with and without sauces or with breads and even soups.

 Toast with "Salud!"

Germany – Oktoberfest Time

Sitting on the cusp of the geographical climate limitations for growing grapes, Germany has 13 wine regions clustered mostly in the southwest corner of the country bordering France. Because of the colder climate, Germany's wine production is devoted primarily to its extraordinary white wines, although the reds are gaining ground and now account for up to 25% of Germany's wine production.

Best bets for pairing with your German fare:

Riesling – With the first plantings dating back to 1435, this crisp, bright white wine is Germany's flagship varietal and is one of the few whites that can age for a considerable time.
Gewürztraminer – A fragrant, flavorful white, this wine has a hint of sweetness. It can be compared to a White Zinfandel. It is best with a highly seasoned and spicy dish.

A German Red? Try a Pinot Noir

Menu Suggestions:

There is always the lusciously wine-marinated Sauerbraten or the typical beer and bratwurst dinner. But, for a change of pace, try a brunch or luncheon treat of Kirschpfannkuchen (*Cherry Pancakes recipe page 9*) served with German sausage and potato salad.

 Toast with "Zum wohl!"

France – A Bastille Day Bash

Long known as "setting the bar" for the quality of wines they produce, France and Italy always run neck and neck for the highest volume of wine production in the world. Although facing stiff international competition, an ideal climate combined with centuries of careful cultivation have given France the commonly held belief that its wines are the best of the best.

Best bets for pairing with your French fare:

Merlot – With a reputation of low acidity and softness, this medium-bodied red is a safe bet with most meals.
Chablis – This white is especially good when pairing it with a dish

having a sour component such as vinaigrette or lemon.

Champagne – This universally adored choice is perfect with most any dish.

Menu Suggestions:

A French theme can lend itself an air of elegant sophistication, but that doesn't mean it needs days of preparation. Try a first course of Onion Soup Gratinee *(recipe page 49)*, a main course of Coq Au Vin *(recipe page 140)* and a delicious Champagne-Lavender Cake *(recipe page 189)* for dessert.

What to wear? Dress as your favorite French chef from this book or fall back on the old, maid outfit. *(French maid, that is!)*

 Toast with "Santé!"

Italy – Create a "Little Italy" at Home

Little ol' Italy, making more than 2,000 wines within its borders, accounts for nearly 30% of the world's wine production. From tip to toe of the boot, wine is produced in every part of Italy.

Best bets for pairing with your Italian fare:

Sangiovese – One of Italy's oldest varietals, it is the main component of Chianti. With medium to high levels of tannins and acidity, it's a perfect match for your red sauce-based dishes.

Pinot Bianco – If looking for an Italian white, this one is crisp, medium-bodied and dry with a light fruitiness.

Chianti – Is there anything better for ambiance than straw-wrapped Chianti bottles and candles?

Menu Suggestions:

There are numerous outstanding Italian recipes included in this book. As our sentimental favorite, we'll have to go for Shari's Signature Lasagna as our recommendation *(recipe page 21)*. Although it takes some time to   prepare, it is beyond compare. Served with a green salad and crusty bread *(don't forget the Italian olive oil and balsalmic vinegar for dipping)*, it is a meal to remember.

 Toast With: "Cin! Cin!"

STRAWBERRIES IN ZABAGLIONE SAUCE

Difficulty: ♟♟♟

Preparation Time: 30 minutes plus chilling time

Yield: 4 servings

20 strawberries
2 tablespoons sugar
1 cup Blush Wine*
1 ounce semi-sweet chocolate, grated

Zabaglione Sauce:

4 egg yolks
1/3 cup sugar
1 teaspoon lemon juice
1/3 cup Blush Wine

1. Place all zabaglione sauce ingredients in top of double boiler. Whisk briskly over hot water. Continue to whisk until mixture takes on the consistency of whipped cream. Remove from heat.

2. Wash strawberries and remove stems. Pat dry, place in a large bowl and set aside.

3. Combine sugar and wine. Mix well and pour over strawberries. Cover and refrigerate at least 4 hours.

4. Place strawberries in a wine glass. Spoon warm zabaglione sauce over the strawberries and top with grated chocolate.

Contributed by Chef Dana Taylor of Los Pinos Ranch Vineyards

Author's Note: We love the name of their Blush; it's called Pinky Tuscandero

WineWisdom

"In water one sees one's own face; but in wine one beholds the heart of another."
~French Proverb~

"Leave the flurry to the masses; take good wine and fill your glasses."
~George H. Boynton, Sr.~

"Wine, the most agreeable of beverages, whether we owe it to Noah who planted the first vine, or to Bacchus who pressed the first grapes, dates from the beginning of the world."
~Anthelme Brillat-Savarin~

"A fine wine lasts a long time in your mouth . . . and in your mind."
~Christian Moueix~

"Let us drink the juice divine, the gift of Bacchus, god of wine."
~Anacreon~

"Let us celebrate the occasion with wine and sweet words."
~Plautus~

"I have taken more out of alcohol than alcohol has taken of me."
~Winston Churchill~

"Wine remains a simple thing, a marriage of pleasure."
~Andre Tchelistcheff~

"Let the poet, inspired by wine, call upon this muse for songs of joy and laughter."
~Propertius~

"Good company, good wine, good welcome, make good people."
~William Shakespeare~

WINE FRUIT CUPS

This dish doubles as either an appetizer or a dessert.

Difficulty: 🍷🍷

Preparation Time: 25 minutes plus chilling time

Yield: 6 servings

1 1/2 cups dry white wine
1 tablespoon lemon juice
1/4 teaspoon salt
1/2 cup sugar
1 1/2 teaspoons anise seed
1 small cinnamon stick
1/2 cup golden seedless raisins
2 nectarines or peaches, sliced
4 purple plums, sliced

1. In a small saucepan, combine the wine, sugar, lemon juice, anise seed, salt and cinnamon stick. Bring to a boil, then turn off heat and cool to room temperature.

2. Combine the raisins, plums and nectarines or peaches in a bowl and strain the cooled wine syrup over them.

3. Cover and refrigerate for several hours, stirring occasionally.

WINE POACHED PEARS WITH CREAM

Difficulty: ♟♟♟

Preparation Time: 1 hour, 15 minutes

Yield: 6 servings

6 whole pears
11/2 cups dry white wine
1 cup light brown sugar (or more, to taste)
12 thin strips of lemon peel
1 teaspoon lemon juice
1 tablespoon butter
1/2 cup light rum, warmed
11/2 cups whipped cream sweetened with vanilla extract to taste

1. Peel, halve and core pears.

2. Place pears, wine, sugar, lemon peel, lemon juice and butter in a shallow pan. Cover with water and poach over low heat until tender, about 45 minutes.

3. When pears are tender, remove and place in a casserole dish. Cook remaining liquid until syrupy, about 10 minutes.

4. Pour sauce over pears. To serve, pour warm rum over the fruit and flambé (see safety notes on page 70). When the flames die out, serve the pears in dessert dishes topped with cold whipped cream.

> "Oh bliss! Bliss and heaven! Oh, it was gorgeousness and gorgeousity made flesh. It was like a bird of rarest-spun heaven metal or like silvery wine flowing in a spaceship, gravity all nonsense now. As I slooshied, I knew such lovely pictures!"
> ~Alex in *A Clockwork Orange* (1971)
>
> "We want the finest wines available to humanity, we want them here, and we want them now!"
> ~Withnail in *Withnail and I* (1987)

MILK

ARTICHOKE TAPANADE DIP

Difficulty: ▮

Preparation Time: 40 minutes

Servings: 6

1 jar artichoke tapenade
1/2 cup good quality mayonnaise
1/2 cup sour cream
8 ounces cream cheese
3 tablespoons Chardonnay
4 ounces goat cheese
1 cup Parmesan cheese
1 clove garlic, minced
Sliced baguette or your favorite crackers

1. Heat oven to 350°.

2. Drain excess oil from the artichoke tapanade. Combine all ingredients, except bread or crackers, in an oven-proof baking dish. Bake for 30 minutes or until heated through. Serve immediately with Chardonnay and the reserved bread.

Contributed by Lambert Bridge Winery

Wine and Cheese, if you please! When pairing the two, consider texture, flavors and sweetness. In general, white wines go better with cheese than red wines. Hard cheeses with a mild flavor match more wines than their soft, ripe or boldly flavored counterparts. The more tannic the red the harder and stronger flavored the cheese should be.

"Hey man, I'm drinking some wine, eating some cheese, and catching some rays; you know . . ."
~Oddball in *Kelly's Heroes* (1970)

BAKED VIDALIA ONIONS IN SHERRY CREAM SAUCE

Difficulty: 🍷🍷
Preparation Time: 35 minutes
Yield: 6 servings

3 cups Vidalia (or other sweet) onions, sliced
1/3 cup Sherry
1 cup light cream or sour cream
1/2 teaspoon salt
1/2 teaspoon pepper
2 eggs, beaten
2 tablespoons pimentos, chopped
4 ounces mushrooms, sliced
3 tablespoons butter
1/2 cup sharp cheddar cheese, grated

1. Heat oven to 350°.

2. Sauté or boil onions until soft. Drain the onions and arrange them in a shallow baking dish.

3. In a bowl, combine Sherry, cream, salt, pepper, eggs, pimentos and mushrooms.

4. Pour mixture over the onions. Dot with butter. Sprinkle with grated cheese, cover and bake for 20 minutes.

BLUE CHEESE CRISPS
Difficulty: ♟
Preparation Time: 15 minutes plus refrigerate overnight
Yield: 1 cup spread

6 ounces blue or Roquefort cheese
4 tablespoons butter, softened
4 tablespoons brandy
5 large red apples
1/2 cup lemon juice
Crackers or melba toasts

1. Mix cheese, butter and brandy in a small bowl. Cover and refrigerate overnight or until needed.

2. Core apples and slice into 1/2-inch slices. Dip in lemon juice to keep from turning brown. To serve, make a tray of apples and breads and spread the cheese mixture on all.

"Now, a clever man would put the poison into his own goblet, because he would know that only a great fool would reach for what he was given. I am not a great fool, so I can clearly not choose the wine in front of you. But you must have known I was not a great fool, you would have counted on it, so I can clearly not choose the wine in front of me . . ."
~Vizzini in *The Princess Bride* (1987)

"It's the same things your whole life. Clean up your room! Stand up straight! Pick up your feet! Take it like a man! Be nice to your sister! Don't mix beer and wine, ever! Oh yeah, and don't drive on the railroad track!"
~Phil Connors in *Groundhog Day* (1993)

Do you know your wine from the Grand Ole United States?

1. Which state has the greatest wine production?
    a.) California
    b.) New York
    c.) Oregon
    d.) Texas

2. Founded in 1839, the oldest, continuously operating winery in the U.S. is Brotherhood Winery. Where is this winery located?
    a.) California
    b.) New York
    c.) Washington
    d.) Texas

3. Oregon's reputation as a wine producing state is spreading rapidly. What is Oregon's flagship wine?
    a.) Cabernet Sauvignon
    b.) Chardonnay
    c.) Riesling
    d.) Pinot Noir

4. What is Washington's first American Viticultural Area (AVA)? The primary grapes planted in this AVA are Chardonnay, Merlot and Cabernet.
    a.) Columbia Valley
    b.) Yakima Valley
    c.) Walla Walla Valley
    d.) Puget Sound

 Solutions on page 241

BRIE, ROQUEFORT AND WILD MUSHROOM FONDUE

Difficulty: ♟♟
Preparation Time: 30 minutes
Yield: 6 - 8 servings

1 1/2 teaspoons olive oil
4 ounces fresh shiitake mushrooms, stemmed, caps diced
1 shallot, minced
1 teaspoon chopped fresh thyme
1 1/2 tablespoons all-purpose flour
12 ounces chilled 60% (double creme) Brie cheese (do not use triple
  creme)
2 ounces chilled Roquefort cheese
1 cup dry white wine
1 (13-ounce) loaf crusty white bread, cut into 1 1/2-inch cubes
Vegetables (such as carrot sticks, blanched broccoli, cauliflower and
  boiled small potatoes)

1. Heat oil in heavy medium skillet over medium-high heat. Add
mushrooms, shallot and thyme; sauté until mushrooms just begin to
soften, about 2 minutes.

2. Place flour in large bowl. Cut rind from Brie; discard rind. Cut Brie
into cubes; drop into flour. Toss to coat; separate cheese cubes.
Crumble Roquefort into same bowl; toss to coat. Place wine in heavy
medium saucepan and bring to simmer over medium heat. Add cheese
by handfuls, stirring until melted after each addition. Continue stirring
until smooth.

3. Stir mushroom mixture into fondue. Season with generous amount
of pepper. Transfer to fondue pot. Set pot over candle or canned heat
burner. Serve with bread and vegetables.

Contributed by Andretti Winery

CHEESE SOUFFLÉ

Difficulty: ♟♟♟
Preparation time: 1 1/2 hours
Yield: 6 servings

3 tablespoons butter or margarine
3 tablespoons all purpose flour
1 teaspoon salt
1/4 teaspoon dry mustard
1/2 cup milk
1/2 cup Chardonnay
1/4 teaspoon hot sauce
1 cup sharp cheddar cheese, grated
4 eggs, separated

1. Heat oven to 300°.

2. Melt butter in a small saucepan. Blend in flour, salt and mustard. Stir in milk and wine and continue cooking until mixture boils and thickens.

3. Add hot sauce and cheese. Reduce heat to low and heat until cheese melts, stirring frequently. Remove from heat.

4. In a bowl, beat egg yolks slightly and add them to the cooked mixture. Beat egg whites until stiff and fold them into the mixture.

5. Turn the mixture into a 2-quart baking dish. Set inside a larger pan of hot water. Bake for 1 hour. Serve immediately.

Buzz on the Vine

Host Your Own Wine-Tasting Party!

Wine tasting parties are festive and fun. They are also simple to plan and host. Here are some recommendations to make your party an event to remember:

Decide whether you wish to focus on red wines, white wines, or sparkling wines. If you plan to taste a mixture of wines, start with the sparkling wines, then move from the lighter whites to the fuller-bodied reds. Since you will want to try several wines of each type offered, it is easier to restrict your tasting to one of these groups. You may want to select a theme for the event, such as International Wines or California Chardonnays.

You may wish to supply all the wine for tasting. In this case, it is fun to offer a low-priced wine, some medium-priced wines and a couple more expensive wines. Another enjoyable option is to ask each guest to bring one of their favorite wines from the chosen category.

Place each bottle in a paper bag and secure bag with tape or rubber band around neck of the bottle. The idea is to disguise the bottle so the taster is not prejudiced by the label or appearance of the bottle. Identify each bottle with a number or some other demarcation so you can differentiate one from another for tasting notes. When the tasting involves white wines, it is common to keep the wine cool in a wine bucket. In this case the bottle will get wet, so you may choose to cover the label with aluminum foil and use rubber bands to keep the cover in place. Another option is to simply decant the wine.

Use clear and clean glassware for your tasting. Color and general appearance of the wine are important aspects of the tasting experience.

Remember to let your red wines breathe before tasting. Older reds generally require more time to breathe than younger reds. You may want to let your white wines breathe for 10 to 15 minutes before tasting.

If you serve hors d'oeuvres during the tasting event, try not to serve anything that would hamper ones ability to taste the wine. Cheese and bread or crackers are a popular choice.

Provide each guest with a wine tasting scoring sheet and pen or pencil for taking notes and recording their reactions to each wine tasted. These notes should be kept private until everyone has completed their tasting. Create a tasting sheet of your own with categories including appearance, bouquet, taste and overall impression or ranking. A sample tasting sheet is shown on the following pages.

Once the tasting has been completed, have guests share their reactions and rankings. After this has been completed, remove the covers from the bottles to reveal the hidden labels. It is always interesting, and often surprising, to see how and why people rank the wines the way they do.

In the end, the best wine is the wine that tastes best to you! Enjoy a wine party with your friends; you won't be disappointed.

WINE TASTING SCORING SHEET

🍷 Date: _____

🍷 Wine Varietal/Theme: _____

🍷 Taster's Name: _____

Directions: With each wine, circle your rating for each of the categories: Appearance, Nose, Taste and Finish. Total Score is the sum of the four scores. A perfect score is 20. Your favorite wine will be the one with the highest Total Score.

Ranking System: The greater score, the better the wine.

	5	4	3	2	1
Appearance	Clear, appropriate color, no haze or cloudiness			Cloudy or murky, color is wrong	
Nose	Diverse, interesting and pleasing scent or smell			Little or no aroma, or unpleasant smell	
Taste	Good balance between sweetness and acidity, variety of flavors			Poor balance, resulting in harsh or unpleasant	
Finish	Taste remaining after swallowing is smooth and rich			Taste ends right away, or aftertaste is unpleasant	

Visit our website at www.thewinepyramid.com to download a single page version of this scoring form.

Wine A Appearance: 1 2 3 4 5 Nose: 1 2 3 4 5 Taste: 1 2 3 4 5 Finish: 1 2 3 4 5 Total Score: _____ Notes: _____	**Wine B** Appearance: 1 2 3 4 5 Nose: 1 2 3 4 5 Taste: 1 2 3 4 5 Finish: 1 2 3 4 5 Total Score: _____ Notes: _____
Wine C Appearance: 1 2 3 4 5 Nose: 1 2 3 4 5 Taste: 1 2 3 4 5 Finish: 1 2 3 4 5 Total Score: _____ Notes: _____	**Wine D** Appearance: 1 2 3 4 5 Nose: 1 2 3 4 5 Taste: 1 2 3 4 5 Finish: 1 2 3 4 5 Total Score: _____ Notes: _____
Wine E Appearance: 1 2 3 4 5 Nose: 1 2 3 4 5 Taste: 1 2 3 4 5 Finish: 1 2 3 4 5 Total Score: _____ Notes: _____	**Wine F** Appearance: 1 2 3 4 5 Nose: 1 2 3 4 5 Taste: 1 2 3 4 5 Finish: 1 2 3 4 5 Total Score: _____ Notes: _____

Wine Ranking:

1st : _____ most favorite   4th: _____

2nd : _____   5th: _____

3rd: _____   6th: _____ least favorite

CHILIES RELLENO CASSEROLE

This casserole may be served as a colorful dinner entree or a delicious brunch dish with fresh fruit and warm tortillas.

Difficulty: ♟♟
Preparation Time: 1 hour
Yield: 6 servings

6 canned whole green chilies
2 cups grated cheddar and jack cheese blend (Mexican style
  works best)
6 eggs, beaten
5-ounce can evaporated milk
1/2 teaspoon salt
1/2 teaspoon ground black pepper
1/4 teaspoon ground red pepper
1/4 cup dry white wine
2 tablespoons flour
Sour cream (optional)
Salsa (optional)

1. Heat oven to 350°.

2. Unfold the chilies and stuff each with about 3 tablespoons of cheese. Refold them and place into a greased baking dish. Top the chilies with the remaining cheese.

3. In a bowl, combine eggs, milk, salt, peppers, wine and flour. Blend well. Pour egg mixture over the chilies.

4. Bake for 45 minutes or until golden brown on top.

5. If desired, top with sour cream and/or salsa before serving.

EASY CHEESY CRAB SPREAD

Difficulty: 🍷
Preparation Time: 25 minutes
Yield: 6 appetizer servings

8 ounces cream cheese, softened
1/4 cup Chardonnay
8 ounces crab meat
2 tablespoons green onion, chopped
1/2 teaspoon horseradish
1/4 teaspoon salt
1/4 teaspoon pepper
1/3 cup pistachios, chopped
Crackers

1. Heat oven to 375°.

2. Blend cream cheese and wine until smooth. Add in crab, onion, horseradish, salt and pepper. Stir to mix well.

3. Put cheese mixture in a small baking dish and top with pistachios. Bake for 15 minutes.

4. To serve, place on a tray with a variety of crackers.

CORKBOARD

The soil of the famed Grand Cru vineyard "Clos de Vougeot" in France's Burgundy region is considered so precious that vineyard workers are required to scrape it from their shoes before they leave for home each night. Man, those French take it seriously.

Portugal, Spain and Italy produce 90% of the world's cork for wine bottles. Cork forests have become reserves for wildlife and in fact harbor some nearly extinct species, including the Iberian lynx in Portugal.

The largest cork tree in the world is in Portugal. It averages more than one ton of raw cork per harvest. That's enough to cork 100,000 bottles.

While there are nearly 400 species of oak, only about 20 are used to make oak barrels. Of the trees that are used, only 5% is suitable for making high grade wine barrels. The average age of a French oak tree harvested for use in wine barrels is 170 years!

The 6 largest European wine producers are Italy, France, Spain, Russia, Germany and Romania.

There is no commercial winery in Tibet.

Most wine grapes grow between 30° and 50° north and between 30° and 40° south. The world's most southerly vineyards are on the South Island of New Zealand near the 45th parallel.

The only continent on Earth that does not produce wine is Antarctica.

GOUDA FONDUE

Difficulty: ❢❢
Preparation Time: 20 minutes
Yield: 8 servings

2 pounds Gouda cheese
1 pound Emmentaler cheese
3/4 bottle Chardonnay
Juice of 1/2 lemon
1 clove garlic, halved
10 tablespoons cornstarch
Pepper from 3 turns of a peppermill

1. Rub the fondue pot with the cut surface of garlic.

2. Coarsely grate the cheeses and mix them together in bowl.

3. Add wine, lemon juice and cornstarch to fondue pot and stir together over medium-high heat. Wait for the cornstarch to begin to thicken.

4. Begin adding cheeses to melt completely. Stir in a figure-eight motion to prevent cheese from getting stringy.

5. Add pepper and cook a bit longer until mixture is smooth and creamy. Transfer the pot to the burner on the table, where the fondue can simmer.

Contributed by Van Ruiten Vineyards

To truly understand terroir, one needs to learn as much as possible about the uniqueness of an area. Study the soil, the climate, the altitude, etc. and the effect all this has on a wine's character. These items vary dramatically from one area to the next and are the basis for wine style diversity. Terroir means that it is technically impossible to make exact copies of the world's great single-vineyard wines. Once one knows the terroir, the challenge is to modify what can and should be improved to deliver the best possible wines.

wine wit

TRUST ME — **NOTHING** CAN GO WRONG... ALL YOU NEED FOR A BLIND TASTING IS **SIX** BOTTLES, **SIX** BAGS AND **SIX** GLASSES

KIKI'S KICKIN' COSTA RICA SAUCE

This sauce is also good over chicken breasts or tilapia fish filets.

Difficulty: ♟♟

Preparation Time: 30 minutes

Yield: 6 servings

1/2 cup butter
Six 4-ounce breakfast steaks
Salt and pepper to taste
1 teaspoon oregano
2 teaspoons garlic salt
1 teaspoon pepper
1/4 cup dry white wine
1 onion, diced
8 ounces mushrooms, sliced
4-ounce can diced jalapeños
4-ounce can diced mild green chilies
1 cup sour cream

1. In a large saucepan or Dutch oven, melt cube of butter. Season steaks with salt and pepper and pan fry in butter until done, about 5 minutes per side. Remove steaks to a platter and keep warm.

2. Season the butter and drippings in the pan with the oregano, garlic salt and 1 teaspoon pepper. Add mushrooms, wine and onion and pan fry until tender, about 10 minutes.

3. Add jalapeños and green chilies and continue cooking for 3 minutes. Stir in sour cream and serve sauce over breakfast steaks.

WINE WORDS

Part One *"Tasting", Continued from Page 68*

🍷 *Luscious* – Rich, ripe, fruity and full-flavored wines can be described as being luscious.

🍷 *Maturity* – Mature is a complimentary term for a wine that is past its youth but before its decline.

🍷 *Meaty* – As the tannin begins allowing the fruit flavors to emerge, this term refers to a substantial and full bodied fruit flavor.

🍷 *Nose* – Again, referring to the smell of the wine. Its two components are the aroma from the grapes and the bouquet from fermentation and aging.

🍷 *Nutty* – In sherries or fine white wines you might find a fine, crisp flavor which is referred to as nutty.

🍷 *Oaky* – As flavor is imparted to a wine from the cask or barrel, a toasty, wood-like or sometimes vanilla flavor and aroma can be presented to a wine.

🍷 *Round* – A wine that is smooth and well developed without any rough edges.

🍷 *Sharp* – This is not necessarily an unpleasant descriptor, but refers to pronounced acid taste on the palate.

🍷 *Short* – When referring to the aftertaste or finish, a wine with none is called short.

🍷 *Continued on Page 161*

MAKE-AHEAD BRUNCH RAMEKINS

Difficulty: ▼
Preparation Time: 15 minutes plus chilling time
Yield: 4 servings

4 slices white bread, crusts removed
Soft butter or margarine
3 eggs
1 1/2 cups half-and-half or milk
1/2 cup Chablis
1/4 teaspoon salt
1/4 teaspoon dry mustard
2 cups Swiss cheese, shredded
2 green onions, finely chopped (include some of the tops for color.)

1. Heat oven to 350°.

2. Spread each bread slice with butter and place into 4 individual baking dishes or ramekins.

3. Beat eggs until foamy and then blend in half-and-half, wine, salt and mustard.

4. Top each bread slice with one quarter of the shredded cheese and one quarter of the egg mixture. Sprinkle chopped onions on top. Cover and chill at least 1 hour or overnight.

5. Bake for 30 minutes. Serve immediately.

In 1998, she became the Wine Institute's first female Chairperson since its establishment in 1934.

    a.) Diane Nury
    b.) Eileen Crane
    c.) Maryann Graf
    d.) Ann Colgin

Solution: a.) Diane Nury. During the same year, Napa Valley Vintners and Sonoma County Wineries Associations in California each elected a woman as president of their respective boards for the first time.

PASTA WITH GORGONZOLA SAUCE

Difficulty: ♟♟
Preparation Time: 25 minutes
Yield: 4 servings

16 ounces dried pasta
3 tablespoons butter
3 tablespoons flour
1 cup milk
1/4 cup white wine
1 clove garlic, peeled and split
1/4 teaspoon paprika
1/4 teaspoon cayenne pepper
6 ounces Gorgonzola cheese, crumbled
Salt and freshly ground pepper, to taste

1. Cook the pasta in a large pot of rapidly boiling, salted water. Drain.

2. While the pasta is cooking, prepare the sauce. Melt the butter in a medium saucepan over a low heat. Add the flour and cook, stirring frequently, 5 minutes over a low heat. The mixture should not brown.

3. Whisk in the milk, wine, garlic, paprika and cayenne pepper. Cook, whisking constantly, over a medium heat until the mixture is thickened and has lost its floury taste, about 10 minutes.

4. Whisk in the cheese. When melted, season the sauce to taste with salt and pepper.

5. Toss the sauce with the cooked pasta.

Contributed by Husch Vineyards

wine wit

SCALLOPS IN WINE CHEESE SAUCE

Consider serving this dish over hot, fluffy rice.

Difficulty: ♟
Preparation Time: 25 minutes
Yield: 8 servings

1 1/2 pounds scallops
1/4 cup dry white wine
1/2 teaspoon salt
1/2 teaspoon cayenne pepper
1/4 cup finely minced onion
3 tablespoons butter
3 tablespoons all purpose flour
1/2 cup half-and-half or whipping cream
1 cup grated Swiss cheese

1. Heat oven to 400°.

2. In a medium saucepan, simmer scallops, wine, salt, cayenne and onion, covered, for approximately 3 minutes. Drain and reserve 1 cup of liquid. Set scallops aside.

3. Melt butter in the saucepan and blend in the flour. Add reserved liquid and half-and-half or cream. Whisk together to make a smooth cream sauce.

4. Add grated cheese and then scallops. Place all into a 1 1/2-quart casserole dish and bake for 12 minutes.

No drips, please. Three methods used to prevent drops of wine from running down the side of the bottle onto easily stained surfaces include a wine collar, drip dickey and napkin.

(Bond is surprised to learn Grant is a double agent.) "Red wine with fish. Well, that should have told me something."
~James Bond in *From Russia with Love* (1963)

WINEWISDOM

"Drink wine, and you will sleep well. Sleep, and you will not sin. Avoid sin, and you will be saved. Ergo, drink wine and be saved."
~Medieval German Saying~

"What though youth gave love and roses, age still leaves us friends and wine."
~Thomas Moore~

"May we never want for wine, nor for a friend to help drink it."
~Anonymous~

"Wine gives great pleasure; and every pleasure is of itself a good."
~Samuel Jackson~

"I often wonder what the vintners buy, one half so precious as the goods they sell."
~Omar Khayyam~

"Wine helps open the heart to reason."
~Jewish Saying~

"The soft extractive note of an aged cork being withdrawn has the true sound of a man opening his heart."
~William S. Benwell~

"I drink when I have occasion, and sometimes when I have no occasion."
~Miguel de Cervantes~

"Sip, swirl, swallow!"
~Anonymous~

CELLAR CHALLENGE

Host a Wine and Cheese Party!

We truly enjoy cheese with our wine, as an appetizer and sometimes for a meal. In fact, we have a wine-bottle shaped cheese board that we serve it on.

Wine and cheese are wonderful partners. And since they are good partners, why not throw a wine and cheese party? If you invite guests, ask each person to bring a bottle of their favorite wine along with their favorite cheese.

This brings us to the big question: Which cheese to serve with which wine? Can you match the pairings below?

Set 1: 1. Blue Cheese/Roquefort   a. Beaujolais
        2. Brie   b. Chardonnay
        3. Cream Cheese   c. Riesling
        4. Feta   d. Sparkling Wine
        5. Monterey Jack   e. Tawny Port
        6. Provolone   f. White Zinfandel

Set 2: 1. Goat Cheese   a. Cabernet Sauvignon
        2. Gouda   b. Chardonnay
        3. Limburger   c. Gewürztraminer, Riesling
        4. Mozzarella   d. Light Red or White
        5. Sharp Cheddar   e. Sparkling Wine
        6. Swiss   f. Who Eats Limburger?

Solutions on page 242

SHERRIED CAMEMBERT WITH GRAPES

Difficulty: 🍷
Preparation Time: 10 minutes plus chilling time
Yield: 4 servings

5 ounces ripe Danish Camembert cheese
1/3 cup dry or cream Sherry
1/3 cup walnuts, finely chopped
Wheat crackers or melba toasts
Grapes

1. Combine cheese with Sherry until smooth and creamy. Shape cheese into a ball, oval, or wedge. Coat the top with walnuts. Chill until firm.

2. Before serving, stand at room temperature for 20 minutes. Serve on a platter with grapes and breads.

Ullage, which comes from the Latin word oculus ("eye"), refers to the air space in a bottle of wine or barrel. In a bottle of wine, the air space is necessary to allow for expansion of the contents due to temperature changes. As wine ferments in a barrel, it soaks into the wood and slowly evaporates. The resulting air can allow bacteria and yeasts to attack the wine, causing undesired fermentations to occur. This is why it is necessary to keep barrels full.

How can you tell if a bottle of wine over 10 years old is drinkable? One way is the ullage.

•High fill- Outstanding storag and probably excellent taste
•Top shoulder- Normal storage and should taste fine
•Low shoulder- Poor storage and probably not drinkable

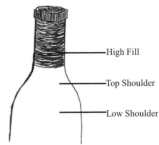

High Fill

Top Shoulder

Low Shoulder

WINE SCORES

This Wine Received a 93!

There is tremendous hype surrounding wine scores. Robert Parker's *The Wine Advocate* journal and *Wine Spectator* magazine both use 100 point rating scales. Others use varying scales, such as a 20 point scale or a scale based on stars. We have friends that buy wine simply because the wine received a high numerical score from an expert wine taster. This begs the question, should wine be purchased based on a third party ranking of the wine?

Advantages: Wine scores can serve as a selection guide when staring at the ominous wall of wine in stores. Scores can help you assess the price and value of the wine you are considering. Finally, when you find a wine critic with tastes similar to yours, recommendations from this critic can simplify the comparison process.

Disadvantages: Everyone has their own unique tastes and preferences. Yours may be different from that of the wine critic. Wine is complex, and a simple score does not provide information about the body, bouquet, flavor and other factors we consider when choosing a wine to drink. Lastly, in some cases wine scores are controlled by commercial interests, which compromises the value of the scale used.

In summary, wine scores are a powerful marketing tool that can lend some guidance and insight into the selection of a fine wine. In the end however, it is your personal taste and not the wine score that matters.

MEAT AND BEANS

AUNT DIANE'S SHERRIED BEEF

Difficulty: 🍷
PreparationTime: 3 hours
Yield: 8 servings

3 pounds stew meat, cubed
2 cans cream of mushroom soup
3/4 cup Sherry
1/2 package dry onion soup mix
1/2 cup water
1/4 teaspoon nutmeg
1/4 teaspoon oregano
Salt and pepper, to taste

1. Heat oven to 375°.

2. Mix all ingredients together in a large casserole dish. Bake uncovered for 2 hours 40 minutes.

3. Serve over noodles or rice. Add green peas if desired.

AUSTRALIAN STEAK MADAGASCAR

Difficulty: ▼▼▼

Preparation Time: 15 minutes

Yield: 2 servings

16-ounce boneless ribeye or strip steak
2 tablespoons olive oil
2 tablespoons brandy or cognac
1/2 cup Shiraz or Syrah
2 tablespoons green peppercorns
3 tablespoons heavy cream or crème fraiche

1. Heat olive oil in a heavy skillet over high heat until it sizzles. Add steak and sear for 1 minute on each side until browned. Reduce heat to medium and cook for another 5 minutes or until done to your liking. Take care not to overcook.

2. *(Please see the flambé safety precautions on page 70 before attempting this step.)* Pour the brandy or cognac over the meat and "flame" with a lighted match, taking care not to singe your eyebrows.

3. Place the meat on a plate and keep it warm while you fashion a quick sauce. Return heat under the skillet to high and pour in the Shiraz or Syrah and green peppercorns, de-glazing the pan by stirring rapidly to scrape up any browned bits of meat.

4. When the liquid has reduced to a thick glaze, take the skillet off the heat. Stir in the cream or crème fraiche and serve over your steak.

Contributed by wineloverspage.com

Author's note: Take time to check out this site. It's great!

BAHIA STYLE MUSSELS IN TANGERINE-COCONUT BROTH

Difficulty: ♟♟♟
Preparation Time: 40 minutes
Yield: 6 servings

2 pounds fresh mussels
1 cup Fume Blanc
1 bay leaf
3 tablespoons extra virgin olive oil
1 cup diced onion
1 teaspoon chopped garlic
1/2 cup basmati rice
1 1/2 cup chopped tomatoes
1 tablespoon tangerine zest
1 Anaheim chili, diced
1 red jalapeño, minced
1 cup chicken stock
1 cup tangerine juice
1 tablespoon chopped fresh parsley
1 tablespoon chopped fresh basil
1 tablespoon chopped fresh cilantro
Salt and pepper, to taste
1 cup coconut milk
Cilantro, for garnish (optional)

1. Steam mussels in wine with bay leaf and 1 cup water until they open. Set aside.

2. In a separate pan, sauté onion, garlic and peppers in oil until soft. Add rice and stir. Add tomatoes, zest, chicken stock and tangerine juice. Cook until rice is soft.

3. Add some of the broth from mussels, herbs, salt and pepper and simmer for 3 minutes. Add coconut milk and then mussels. Bring to a boil just before serving.

4. To serve, place mussels in bottom of the bowl and cover with broth. Garnish with more cilantro if desired.

Contributed by Chef Robin Lehnhoff of Lake Sonoma Winery

CELLAR CHALLENGE

Do you know your world wine regions?
Try this expert level true/false quiz.

_____ 1. The Vinho Verde wine producing region is in Portugal.

_____ 2. Alsace, Burgundy, Corsica and Loire Valley are all French wine regions.

_____ 3. The Veneto region of Italy is known mainly for Chianti.

_____ 4. Cape Winelands in South Africa boasts more vineyard acreage than anywhere else in the world.

_____ 5. Tavel is a Rosé wine and area in Southern Rhône.

_____ 6. The most widely planted grape in New Zealand is Sauvignon Blanc.

_____ 7. Half of the Rosé wine made in France comes from the Provence region.

_____ 8. To wash down your seafood in Spain you order Manzanilla, which is a type of Sherry.

_____ 9. The Argentine region of Mendoza is nestled in the foothills of the snow-capped Andes.

_____ 10. Ice wine, an intensely flavored wine made from grapes harvested after the first winter frost, is Southern Ontario, Canada's greatest claim to wine fame.

Solutions on page 242

BUZZ ON THE VINE

C elebrity has its Advantages!

 If you want to make a small fortune in the wine business, you need to start out with a large fortune. This statement is often made jokingly, however there is a lot of truth to it. Starting a winery from scratch will cost millions and may take years to begin generating revenue. First, you must build the winery and plant the vines. Then, you will need to spend several years tending the vines until they begin to produce fruit that will allow you to make quality wines. Most people simply can't afford the tremendous financial outlay and required wait period. Is there a shortcut to this process?

Enter the celebrity winemakers! A growing number of celebrities are putting their names and images on wine. Fans are willing to pay premium prices for these wines. There isn't the traditional wait period for a winemaker or winery to develop a reputation for quality in the marketplace. The good news is that they are producing some very good wines.

The dean of celebrity winemakers is movie director Francis Ford Coppola, who owns Rubicon Vineyards in Napa and a vineyard in Sonoma. As a wine enthusiast since his early days in New York, his passion drove him to become a winemaker. In 1975, he used earnings from *The Godfather* (1972) to purchase a large share of the Inglenook winery in Napa Valley.

Actor/comedian Robin Williams owns a 224-acre vineyard in the Mt. Veeder area. He and Robert de Niro are co-owners of Rubicon Vineyards with Coppola.

Just down the road in Napa, champion racecar driver Mario Andretti runs the Andretti Winery. Mario's interest in winemaking was sparked when a commemorative wine was produced in his honor in 1994. The Andretti Winery was established in 1996. *(recipes pages 29 and 98)*

Santa Barbara's Santa Ynez Valley is where Fess Parker, former Davy Crockett and Daniel Boone television star, has owned Fess Parker Winery and Vineyard since 1987.

Vince Neil, of heavy metal band Mötley Crüe, started a wine label in 2005 called Vince Vineyards.

Music legend Bob Dylan has joined forces with Antonio Terni of Italy to produce the first bottles of his Planet Waves signature label.

Greg Norman Estates, with vineyard locations in California and Australia, is owned by golf great Greg "Great White Shark" Norman. Other golfers including Ernie Els and David Frost also have their own wines.

In 2004, rock 'n roll superstar Sir Cliff Richard celebrated the opening of his winery in Portugal's Algarve.

Koala Blue, founded in 1983 by Olivia Newton-John and Pat Farrar, creates wines that are characteristically Australian.

Actor Sam Neill (*Jurassic Park*, etc.) owns Two Paddocks, a winery in the Central Otago region of his native New Zealand, where he produces Pinot Noir wines.

B.R. Cohn Winery offers the "Doobie Red" Series. This limited production Doobie Brothers series features their album covers on the labels: "The Doobie Brothers", "Toulouse Street" and "The Captain and Me".

BAM! Chef/restaurateur Emeril Lagasse and Fetzer Vineyards teamed to produce Emeril's Classics, a line of wines from California.

Sting produces wine for his family and friends at a vineyard he owns in Italy.

The Celebrity Wine Party is alive and well. Are they hobbyists or dedicated winemakers? If the wine is good and their name helps it sell, we're all for it. Salud!

wine wit

BEEF WITH MUSHROOMS

Difficulty: ♉♉♉
Preparation Time: 3 hours
Yield: 8 servings

2 pounds stew meat, trimmed of fat and cut into 1 1/2-inch cubes
1-3 tablespoons olive oil
1 large onion, chopped
6 cloves garlic, minced
Flour
Salt and finely ground black pepper
1 pound white mushrooms, sliced
1-1 1/2 ounces dried porcini mushrooms
2 cups beef broth
2 cups Zinfandel

1. Heat oven to 350°.

2. Soak dried mushrooms in hot water for 20 minutes. Strain and rinse mushrooms, reserving soaking water.

3. Heat Dutch oven to medium-high. Pour 1/2 tablespoon of olive oil into pan. Add onion and sauté for 10 minutes. Add garlic and sauté 2 more minutes.

4. Scoop out onion mixture and set aside. Add 1 tablespoon olive oil and heat to medium-high. Roll beef cubes in mixture of flour, pepper and salt (to taste). Add beef cubes to pan in batches and brown on all sides. Add more olive oil if needed. Take meat out and set aside.

5. Add white mushrooms, porcini mushrooms and soaking liquid to pan and sauté for 5 minutes. Add onions and beef to pan. Pour in beef broth and Zinfandel. Secure lid and put in oven for 1-2 hours—the longer the better. Check halfway through to add liquid if necessary. Serve over pasta, polenta or rice.

Contributed by Pedroncelli Winery and Vineyards

BOEUF À LA NIÇOISE

Difficulty: ❢❢❢❢❢

Preparation Time: 4 1/2 hours plus 12 hours marinating time and 24 hours resting time

Yield: 6 servings

3-4 pound boneless rump or round of beef, trimmed and cut
  into 2-inch cubes
Salt and pepper
4 tablespoons olive oil
3 large onions, chopped
1 carrot, sliced
1 celery stalk, chopped
3 cups Syrah
1 garlic clove, peeled
1 bouquet garni
1/2 cup lean salt pork, diced
2 garlic cloves, crushed
6 small white onions, peeled
2 tomatoes, chopped
1 small piece of pork rind
2 teaspoons thyme
1 clove
Four 2-inch pieces of orange rind
6 carrots, sliced
1/2 cup Niçoise olives or pitted, oil-cured olives
2 tablespoons parsley, finely chopped
1 cup Parmesan or Swiss cheese, grated

1. Rub beef cubes with 1 teaspoon salt. Set aside in large bowl.

2. Heat 3 tablespoons of the olive oil in large, cast-iron skillet. Add chopped onions, carrot and celery and sauté gently for 5 minutes. Stir in the wine, garlic clove, bouquet garni, salt and pepper. Cook for 20 minutes.

3. Let liquid cool, then pour over meat. Cover and marinate in refrigerator overnight.

4. Remove meat from marinade with slotted spoon and dry with paper towels. Do not discard marinade.

5. Heat 1 tablespoon of the olive oil in cast-iron pan. Sauté salt pork gently for 5 minutes. Add beef and cook for 10 minutes, browning beef on all sides.

6. Add crushed garlic and cook for 10 minutes. Add white onions, tomatoes, pork rind, thyme, clove, orange rind, salt, pepper and the marinade. Scrape bottom of pan with spoon, lower the flame and simmer, covered, for 2 hours.

7. Add carrots and cook for 30 minutes; do not overcook the carrots. Refrigerate for 24 hours.

8. Remove fat. Discard bouquet garni and pork and orange rinds. Add black olives and sprinkle with parsley and cheese.

Contributed by Chef Max Duley of Peju Province Winery

BROILED SALMON IN WINE BUTTER

Difficulty: 🍷🍷
Preparation Time: 20 minutes
Yield: 8 servings

1 1/2 cups dry white wine
3 tablespoons minced shallots or green onions
3 tablespoons whipping cream
1 1/2 cups unsalted butter, chilled and cut into small pieces
Juice of 1 lemon
Salt and pepper to taste
8 salmon steaks

1. Boil wine and shallots in a small, heavy saucepan until liquid is reduced to 2 tablespoons. Remove from heat and whisk in cream and two pieces of butter.

2. Over low heat, whisk in remaining butter one piece at a time. Strain the sauce, season with salt and pepper and add lemon juice.

3. Broil salmon steaks until lightly pink and flaky. Spoon sauce over steaks and serve immediately.

"To the Three Great Commanders:
May we always be under the orders of
General Peace, General Plenty,
and General Prosperity."
– Unknown

BRUCE THOMAS' MARINATED TRI-TIP

Difficulty: ♈

Preparation Time: 30 minutes plus marinating time

Yield: 4-6 servings

One whole tri-tip
Yoshida's gourmet sauce (or other marinade)
6 sprigs fresh rosemary
1/2 teaspoon pepper
2 cloves fresh garlic, chopped
1/4 cup Cabernet Sauvignon

1. Place whole tri-tip in gallon size zippered plastic bag and pour in enough gourmet sauce to coat meat. Add rosemary, pepper, chopped garlic and wine. Leave in refrigerator overnight, turning occasionally.

2. Grill until medium rare or to preferred doneness.

Contributed by Chef Bruce Thomas of Mill Creek Vineyards and Winery

---

Remember the three P's when selecting wines from your local market or wine merchant: price, pairing and preference.

Price: Many excellent wines are priced in the $10 - $15 range. Ask for recommendations and look for discounts on the wines you enjoy. You don't need to spend a bundle to enjoy great wine.

Preference: Try a wide variety of wines to determine your preferences. Keep tasting notes on each wine to aide in the selection of future wines. When entertaining guests, you may want to select starter wines that appeal to a broader audience. A Chablis or Chardonnay for whites and a soft Merlot or Pinot Noir for reds tend to be good selections.

Pairing: Purchase wine that goes well with the intended event or meal. When pairing wine with a meal consider flavor interactions, whether fare is heavy or light, and acidity of the food. Regardless of suggestions, select wine that you will enjoy.

CAFÉ CHAMPAGNE SEAFOOD CIOPPINO

Difficulty: ♟♟♟
Preparation Time: 1 hour and 15 minutes
Yield: 6 servings

Sauce:

1 tablespoon garlic, minced
1 tablespoon shallots, minced
1/2 tablespoon ginger, minced
2 tablespoons olive oil
1 bay leaf
1 tablespoon fresh basil, minced
1 tablespoon fresh cilantro, minced
1 tablespoon Italian parsley, minced
2 cups Chardonnay
1 cup clam juice or fish stock
Two 14-ounce cans diced tomatoes
1/2 teaspoon salt
1/2 teaspoon sugar

Cioppino:

1/4 cup olive oil
12 large shrimp, peeled and deveined
8 ounces sea scallops
8 ounces cooked Dungeness crab meat
8 ounces cooked lobster meat, diced
8 ounces white fish such as halibut, diced
12 fresh clams

1. For sauce, sauté garlic, shallots and ginger in oil about 2 minutes. Add bay leaf, salt and sugar. Stir together about one minute until mixed thoroughly. Add wine, tomatoes and juice or stock. Simmer one hour to develop flavor.

2. For Cioppino, heat oil in large pot over high flame. Add shrimp, scallops, white fish and clams. Sauté 1-2 minutes.

3. Add fresh herbs to sauce, then add the sauce to seafood mixture. Simmer 4-5 minutes until clams open. Add lobster and crab to sauce and serve.

Contributed by Thornton Winery

CHICKEN MARSALA

Serve this classic with buttered pasta and a green salad.

Difficulty: 🍷🍷
Preparation Time: 20 minutes
Yield: 2 servings

2 boneless, skinless chicken breasts
2 tablespoons butter
6 large mushrooms, sliced
1 cup Marsala wine
1/2 teaspoon salt
1/4 teaspoon pepper
1 teaspoon lemon juice
3 green onions, chopped
2 teaspoons fresh parsley, chopped

1. Place chicken breasts between sheets of wax paper and pound to 1/4-inch thickness.

2. Melt butter in a medium skillet. Add chicken and cook over low heat until each side is golden brown and tender. Remove chicken to a platter and keep warm.

3. Add next 6 ingredients to the skillet. Cook until mushrooms are tender. Pour wine mixture over the chicken breasts and sprinkle with parsley.

WINE WISDOM

"Wine is the intellectual part of a meal, meats are merely the material part."
~Alexander Dumas~

"Over a bottle of wine, many a friend is found."
~Yiddish Proverb~

"To the corkscrew – a useful key to unlock the storehouse of wit, the treasury of laughter, the front door of friendship, and the gate of a pleasant folly."
~W. E. P. French~

"A roast without a bottle of wine is like a kiss from a man without a mustache."
 ~La Togna (Italian Grandmother of Angelo Pellegrini)~

"Champagne with foaming whirls, as white as Cleopatra's melted pearls."
~Lord Byron~

"All I want out of wines is to enjoy them."
~Ernest Hemingway~

"Fish without wine is like an egg without salt."
 ~Auguste Escoffier~

"Here's to the good time I must have had."
~Anonymous~

"An old wine bibber, having been smashed in a railway collision, some wine was poured on his lips to revive him. 'Pauillac, 1873', he murmured, and died."
~Ambrose Bierce~

"Wine and women – may we always have a taste for both."
~Oliver Wendell Holmes~

". . . So may I, everytime I think of cheese, be moved to take a drink! Lackey, more wine!"
~Saint-Amant~

CHICKEN PASTA PICATTA WITH SPINACH AND RED BELL PEPPERS

"Dinner is the best time of the day. When you serve wine, you don't eat dinner in 10 minutes. Dinner becomes a ritual over which conversation and ideals evolve . . . real quality time." -Gloria Retzlaff, Retzlaff Winery

Difficulty: ♟♟♟
Preparation Time: 40 minutes
Yield: 4 servings

1/2 pound pasta, such as penne, bow ties or shells, uncooked
1 pound boneless, skinless chicken cut into strips
4 tablespoons olive oil
1 large sweet red bell pepper, sliced into 2-inch strips
2 cups spinach leaves, cleaned and destemmed
1/2 cup sliced green onions
1/2 cup Sauvignon Blanc
2 tablespoons lemon juice
2 cloves garlic, minced
1/4 teaspoon garlic salt
1/4 teaspoon freshly ground black pepper
1/3 cup chopped fresh parsley
1 tablespoon capers with a little juice
1/4 cup freshly grated Parmesan cheese

1. Cook pasta according to package directions. Drain and rinse with cold water.

2. In a small saucepan, sauté the chicken strips in 2 tablespoons of the olive oil until the chicken turns white, about 2 minutes. Add the bell pepper strips, spinach and green onions and sauté 2 minutes more.

3. Add the white wine, lemon juice, garlic, garlic salt, pepper, 1/4 cup of the parsley and capers. Stir to mix well and cook mixture for 1-2 minutes.

4. Toss chicken mixture with cooked pasta. Add remaining olive oil, top with remaining chopped parsley and sprinkle with grated Parmesan. Serve hot as a main course, appetizer, or luncheon salad.

Contributed by Retzlaff Estate Winery

BUZZ ON THE VINE

Tonic Time: Wine and Your Health

Although the health benefits of drinking wine in moderation have been long known, Americans didn't jump on the bandwagon until 1991. That fall, *60 Minutes* aired a segment they called The French Paradox. In it, they outlined how the French people have one of the lowest heart attack rates in the world in spite of the fact that they eat inexcusable amounts of high fat, cholesterol-laden foods and exercise little. The "X" factor seemed to be their moderate daily consumption of red wine.

The segment caused such a stir that within one month after its broadcast, sales of red wine soared up 40% (2.5 million bottles). Countless scientific research projects were launched, and are on-going, to determine the effects of drinking wine on our hearts, lungs, brains, bones and more.

In the case of wine, as opposed to other types of alcohol, much of the health benefits are attributed to antioxidants. Antioxidants inhibit the oxidation in the blood that is linked to clogged arteries, blood clot formation and tumor growth. The antioxidant that is prevalent in red wine is called resveratrol. It is produced in plants as a response to stress. Because grapes are harvested when the vines are dehydrated and fighting hard to survive, the resveratrol level is considerably higher in grape skins than most other fruits and vegetables. Recent studies at UC Davis also tout the benefits of another antioxidant in wine called saponins.

Here are some brief highlights of more than 400 studies showing that moderate drinkers live longer:

Heart Disease – Drinking wine increases the level of HDL, or good cholesterol, in the body. HDL flushes excess fat from the blood. Additionally, wine has an anticoagulation effect. This makes blood less likely to clot, therefore reducing the risk of heart disease and ischemic strokes.

Osteoporosis – The denser the bone, the stronger and less likely it is to break. A recent London study indicates that moderate drinkers' blood, urine and x-rays showed significantly denser bones at both the spine and the hip compared to their non-drinking twins.

Alzheimer's and Dementia – Researchers found that moderate drinkers scored higher on tests for cognitive skills including math, intelligence, vocabulary and memory. Results showed a reduced risk of developing Alzheimer's Disease and dementia. The researchers attributed their findings to a greater flow of blood to the brain caused by moderate alcohol consumption.

Prostate Cancer – Again, it's resveratrol cited with the ability to block enzymes that promote tumor development. A study on www.prostatecancernews.org found wine consumption can reduce the risk of prostate cancer up to 50%. Resveratrol also helps curtail the number of cell divisions that lead to cancer.

Diabetes in Women – In the 2002 Journal of American Medicine, researchers disclosed that women in post-menopausal years who consumed alcohol had insulin levels 20% lower than their non-drinking counterparts. The Harvard School of Public Health's study of 100,000 women over 14 showed moderate, regular drinkers to have a 58% lower risk of developing diabetes.

Diet Friendliness – Wine is great for dieters because it's low-carb and fat free. A recent study also indicated that the resveratrol in wine stimulates the activity of a gene called SIRTI, which reduces the growth of new fat cells and increases the use of existing fat cells. (Maybe all those thin, French runway models have known this all along.)

CHICKEN SAUTÉ WITH ARTICHOKES AND SUN-DRIED TOMATOES

Difficulty: ♟♟
Preparation Time: 35 minutes
Yield: 6 servings

6 large boneless, skinless chicken breasts
Plain flour
Dash salt
Dash cayenne pepper
1/2 tablespoon oil
4 ounces pancetta or bacon, chopped
1/2 cup Chardonnay
14 ounces artichoke hearts, drained and halved
2 ounces sun-dried tomatoes in oil, drained and sliced
1 tablespoon sage, finely chopped
Salt and freshly ground black pepper

1. Season flour with salt and cayenne pepper.

2. Trim chicken breasts of any fat and cut into bite sized pieces. Toss into the seasoned flour and shake off any excess. Put on a platter in a single layer.

3. Heat oil in a large frying pan. Add pancetta or bacon and fry until brown. Remove from pan with tongs and keep warm.

4. Add chicken to the hot pan and fry, turning, until golden brown and cooked through. About 10 minutes. Keep warm with the pancetta.

5. Add the Chardonnay to the pan and bring to a boil. Reduce by boiling rapidly until syrupy.

6. Return the meats to the pan. Add the artichoke hearts, sun-dried tomatoes and sage. Reheat and season to taste with salt and pepper.

wine wit

RECENT STUDIES HAVE SUGGESTED THAT MODERATE CONSUMPTION OF WINE COUPLED WITH REGULAR EXERCISE MAY LEAD TO LONGER AND HEALTHIER LIVES AMONG RATS

COQ AU VIN

Difficulty: ❦❦❦❦❦

Preparation Time: 2 hours plus marinating time
Yield: 8 servings

2 whole chickens, quartered
4 carrots, diced
2 onions, diced
2 stalks celery, diced
1 quart red wine
2 bay leaves
1 teaspoon minced garlic
1/2 gallon brown sauce (demi-glaze)
1 cup button mushrooms
8 ounces fresh or frozen pearl onions
1 cup pancetta or bacon, diced

1. Marinate quartered chickens in wine with carrots, celery, onions, bay leaves and garlic overnight (12 hours).

2. Heat oven to 375°. Separate meat, vegetables and wine into 3 bowls.

3. Sauté pancetta or bacon in stock pot or roasting pan until golden. Remove.

4. Sauté chicken until golden and then add marinated vegetables and wine. Cook to reduce wine to 1/2, approximately 10 minutes.

5. Add brown sauce, pearl onions, mushrooms and bacon. Bake for 1 hour. Serve warm.

Contributed by Chef Didier Poirier of 71 Palm Restaurant

EASY BAKED SALMON

Difficulty: ❢
Preparation Time: 40 minutes plus marinating time
Yield: 6 servings

2 1/2 pounds wild salmon fillets
Sea salt and pepper

Marinade:

3/4 cup brown sugar
2 cups soy sauce
2 tablespoons lemon juice
1 teaspoon crushed garlic
1 tablespoon minced ginger
2 tablespoons Syrah

1. Rinse salmon and season with sea salt and pepper.

2. Whisk together all marinade ingredients in mixing bowl. Pour over salmon and marinate for 6-8 hours or overnight for best flavor.

3. Heat oven to 350°.

4. Bake for 30 minutes or just until fish flakes easily.

Contributed by Firestone Vineyard

Wine is all about the balance; the balance of fruit, tannins, acidity and alcohol. When cooking with wine, it is a balancing act to match the right wine with the right food. And to make a special event memorable, one needs to balance the wine with the occasion.

EGGS WITH LOX

Double or triple ingredients as necessary for the number of servings desired.

Difficulty: ♟

Preparation Time: 15 minutes

Yield: 4 servings

6 eggs
3 tablespoons smoked salmon (lox)
1/2 small onion, diced
1 tablespoon green pepper, diced
1/4 cup white wine
1/4 teaspoon salt
1/4 teaspoon pepper

In a skillet, combine all ingredients and mix well. Cook, stirring constantly, until eggs are set, approximately 8 minutes.

GLAZED DUCK WITH PLUM SAUCE

Difficulty: ♦♦♦♦

PreparationTime: 4 hours

Yield: 4-6 servings

5-pound duck
1 teaspoon salt
1/2 teaspoon pepper
1 onion, sliced
1 celery stalk, sliced
3/4 cup Port wine
17-ounce jar purple plums
1/2 bay leaf
6 whole cloves
2 tablespoons red wine vinegar
4 teaspoons cornstarch
1 tablespoon water
Dash salt

1. Heat oven to 325°.

2. Rub body of duck with salt and pepper.

3. Reserve one slice of onion for sauce. Place remaining onion, celery and 1/4 cup of wine inside duck. Truss and place on rack in a roasting pan. Roast for 3 hours, pouring off fat periodically.

4. To prepare sauce, drain and reserve syrup from plums. Add enough water to make 1 cup of syrup. Combine syrup, remaining wine, onion slice, bay leaf, cloves and vinegar in saucepan. Simmer 5 minutes on low heat.

5. Blend cornstarch with 1 tablespoon water and stir into the sauce. Cook until clear and thick, stirring constantly.

6. Strain, reserving sauce. Add dash of salt and then set aside 1/2 cup of sauce for glaze. Combine remaining sauce with strained plums.

7. After roasting for 3 hours, brush duck with reserved glaze and continue roasting for 20 more minutes, basting two times. Reheat sauce and serve with the carved duck.

GRILLED LAMB CHOPS

Difficulty: ❢
Preparation Time: 30 minutes plus 24 hours marinating time
Yield: 4 servings

8 loin lamb chops

Marinade:

2 cloves garlic, minced
1 cup Burgundy or Cabernet Sauvignon
1/2 cup salad oil
2 tablespoons soy sauce
2 tablespoons red wine vinegar
2 teaspoons sugar
1 teaspoon salt
1 teaspoon Accent seasoning
1 teaspoon marjoram
1 teaspoon rosemary

1. Combine all marinade ingredients. Place chops in glass pan and pour marinade over them. Marinate in refrigerator, covered, for 24 hours, turning periodically and spooning sauce over the top.

2. Grill chops over hot coals or medium heat gas until done to taste, basting with the marinade.

". . . the odour of Burgundy, and the smell of French sauces, and the sight of clean napkins and long loaves, knocked as a very welcome visitor at the door of our inner man."
~Jerome K. Jerome *Three Men in a Boat* (1975)

"Ah. Fortune smiles. Another day of wine and roses. Or, in your case, beer and pizza!"
~Two-Face in *Batman Forever* (1995)

"Dynamite? It's like wine, it only gets better with age."
~Tracker Lewis Gates in *Last of the Dogmen* (1995)

GRILLED TRI-TIP WITH GORGONZOLA BUTTER

Difficulty: 🍷🍷
Preparation Time: 20 minutes plus marinating time
Yield: 8 servings

1 cup whiskey
1 cup dry white wine
2 tablespoons Herbes de Provence
1/2 cup crushed, roasted garlic or 2 tablespoons garlic paste
1/2 cup extra virgin olive oil
4-pound tri-tip roast
5 tablespoons butter
5 tablespoons Gorgonzola cheese

1. Mix whiskey, wine, herbs, garlic and oil for marinade. Marinate meat in this for at least two hours. Reserve liquid.

2. Grill tri-tip on gas or charcoal grill to desired doneness, basting often with marinade.

3. With a fork, mash together the butter and Gorgonzola cheese until well blended.

4. When done, slice the roast on a bias and top each serving with a tablespoon of the butter/cheese mixture.

Contributed by Mount Palomar Winery

CORKBOARD

The word wine comes from the Latin word *vinum* referring to both wine and vine.

About 93 percent of households in Denmark consume wine, the highest consumption of all countries. French homes follow with about 85 percent.

Vineyard acreage in Turkey is nearly double that of the United States.

The largest wine cellars in the world are near Capetown, South Africa. Located in the center of their wine district, they cover an area of 25 acres and have a capacity of 36 million gallons. The largest blending vats have a capacity of nearly 55,000 gallons.

In Russia, when invited to a home, it is proper social etiquette for a guest to bring a gift. Acceptable gifts include a bottle of wine or some chocolate, but nothing too expensive.

Mead, a wine made from honey, is the national drink of Poland. (Some proclaim Vodka as the national drink.)

The word "ton" is derived from a tun, a wine barrel. Its name comes from the French "tonnerre", or "thunder", the sound wine barrels make when rolled.

On July 5th, 2001, a dinner for six diners at Petrus in London cost £44,007 ($62,000 US). The bill included 5 bottles of wine: 1947 Chateau Petrus vintage claret worth £12,300 ($17,368), 1945 Chateau Petrus at £11,600 ($16,379), 1946 Chateau Petrus cost £9,400 ($13,273), 1900 Chateau d'Yquem dessert wine cost £9,200 ($12,990) and 1982 bottle of Montrachet was £1,400 ($1,977.00).

GULF COAST CEVICHE

Ceviche is good served in avocado halves, with warmed pita bread, or on top of finely shredded lettuce. Appetizer or main course — your choice!

Difficulty: 🍷🍷
Preparation Time: 15 minutes plus 24 hours chilling time
Yield: 4 quarts

2 medium onions
3 fresh jalapeños
1 bunch cilantro
2 cups lime juice
1 cup olive oil
1 cup dry white wine
2 tablespoons seasoned salt
3 pounds flounder or redfish cut into bite sized pieces or 3 pounds bay scallops
6 ripe tomatoes, cut into bite-sized pieces

1. Place onions, jalapeños and cilantro into a food processor and chop. Add lime juice, olive oil, wine and salt. Mix thoroughly.

2. Stir fish and tomatoes into lime juice mixture and pour all into a glass container. Marinate in the refrigerator for 24 hours, stirring occasionally.

"Here's to the Health
Of those we Love the best: Our noble selves."
– Unknown

HAM AND SAUSAGE JAMBALAYA

Difficulty: ❢
Preparation Time: 45 minutes
Yield: 8 servings

2 cups smoked sausage, sliced
1 cup onion, finely chopped
3/4 cup bell pepper, chopped
1 garlic clove, chopped
2 cups cooked ham, chopped
1/2 cup dry white wine
16-ounce can diced tomatoes
1 teaspoon salt
1/2 teaspoon thyme
1/4 teaspoon basil
1/4 teaspoon marjoram
1/4 teaspoon paprika
1/2 teaspoon Tabasco sauce
2 tablespoons fresh parsley, chopped
1 cup long grain converted rice

1. Sauté sausage in a large saucepan for 10 minutes. Remove and drain on paper towels.

2. Add onion, pepper and garlic to drippings in pan. Sauté for 5 minutes. Stir in the sausage, ham, wine, undrained tomatoes, salt, thyme, basil, marjoram, paprika and Tabasco. Bring to a boil, then reduce heat to low.

3. Add parsley and rice. Mix well. Simmer, covered, for 30 minutes.

Color Me . . . If You Can

Identify the wine grapes from the list below as Red or White. Don't be blue if you aren't able to identify them all correctly; they are difficult!

1. Ramisco	16. Aglianico
2. Furmint	17. Fiano
3. Bastardo	18. Graciano
4. Tannat	19. Kerner
5. Mauzac	20. Prosecco
6. Mencia	21. Carignan
7. Colombard	22. Verdelho
8. Voignier	23. Parellada
9. Roussanne	24. Corvina
10 Gaglioppo	25. Canaiolo
11. Freisa	26. Garganega
12. Marzemino	27. Teroldego
13. Sultana	28. Primotivo
14. Zweigelt	29. Cortese
15. Sagrantino	30. Mencia

Can you unscramble the name for these common grape varieties?

1. Olemtr	6. Necinh Aclbn
2. Ebnercta	7. Glirsine
3. Niopt Iron	8. Lisemoln
4. Gsavoisene	9. Ncahdnorya
5. Haysr	10. Tcmsau

Solutions on page 243

149

HEARTY BLACK BEAN SOUP

Difficulty: ♥♥
Preparation Time: 1 hour
Yield: 6 servings

2 tablespoons olive oil
1/4 cup Sherry or Marsala
2 medium onions, chopped
1 15-ounce can whole peeled tomatoes, chopped (or use fresh, peeled and chopped)
3 cloves garlic, chopped
45 ounces black beans, soaked overnight (or 3 cans)
Salt and pepper, to taste
1 1/4 teaspoon dried oregano
1 1/4 teaspoon cumin
1/2 teaspoon dried thyme
14 1/2 ounces vegetable broth
Grated cheese (cheddar or gorgonzola)
Sour cream
Cilantro

1. Heat the olive oil in a 3-quart saucepan or large pot. Sauté onions over medium heat until transparent. Add garlic and sauté until softened.

2. Stir in beans, oregano, thyme, broth, Sherry (or Marsala) and tomatoes. Simmer, covered, for 45 minutes, or until beans are soft. Season with salt and pepper.

3. Ladle into serving bowls and top with grated cheese, sour cream and cilantro.

Contributed by Oakstone Winery

HUNTER'S STYLE SPRING LAMB STEW

Difficulty: 🍷🍷
Preparation Time: 2 hours
Yield: 6 servings

4 tablespoons olive oil
3 pounds lamb stew meat
2 onions, chopped
2 tablespoons garlic, chopped
1 teaspoon crushed chili flakes
2 tablespoons dry oregano
2 cups Zinfandel
1/2 cup chicken, lamb, or veal stock
2 cups artichoke hearts
2 tablespoons anchovy paste
Freshly ground black pepper to taste
Splash of balsamic vinegar
Kosher salt to taste

1. In heavy sauté pan, salt and pepper lamb and sauté in oil over high heat. Remove from pan and set aside.

2. Add onions, garlic, oregano and chili flakes to pan. When soft, add wine to de-glaze pan.

3. Add lamb back to the pot and add stock. Cook for 11/2 hours or until meat is tender.

4. Add in artichoke hearts, black pepper and anchovy paste. Add balsamic and salt to taste to lift the flavor of the stew.

Contributed by Chef Robin Lehnhoff of Kenwood Vineyards

JAMBALAYA AND CREOLE SEASONING

Difficulty: ♟♟♟
Preparation Time: 1 hour
Yield: 8 servings

3 chicken breasts, diced
1 1/2 pounds Rock shrimp, rinsed and roughly chopped
2 tablespoons olive oil
10 ounces andouille sausage, diced
1 yellow onion, small dice
2 green bell peppers, small dice
4 celery ribs, small dice
2 jalapeño peppers, minced (optional)
5 garlic cloves, minced
2 bay leaves
1 cup Zinfandel
2 cups canned, peeled, diced tomatoes
1/2 teaspoon Worcestershire sauce
1 teaspoon hot sauce
1 1/2 cups rice
6 cups chicken stock
Salt and pepper, to taste

Creole Seasoning:
2 1/2 tablespoons paprika
2 tablespoons kosher salt
2 tablespoons garlic powder
1 tablespoon fresh ground black pepper
1 tablespoon onion powder
1 tablespoon cayenne pepper
1 tablespoon dried oregano
1 tablespoon dried thyme

1. Combine chicken and shrimp with enough Creole Seasoning to lightly coat.

2. In a large pot, heat olive oil until it is smoking hot. Add andouille and cook to render a little of its fat. Remove the sausage, keeping the pot on the fire, add onions, bell peppers and celery, stir.

3. Once the vegetables have started to soften, add garlic, jalapeño

peppers, bay leaves, and stir. De-glaze pan with Zinfandel, scraping all the sausage drippings off the bottom of the pan. Add tomatoes, Worcestershire and hot sauce. Stir in rice and slowly add the stock.

4. Reduce heat to medium and cook until rice absorbs liquid and becomes tender, stirring occasionally, about 20 minutes.

5. When rice is just tender, add shrimp, chicken and the reserved andouille. Cook until meat is done, about 10 minutes. Season to taste with salt, pepper and Creole Seasonings.

Contributed by Lambert Bridge Winery

How many U.S. states produce wine?

    a.) 30
    b.) 35
    c.) 40
    d.) 50

Solution: (d) All 50 states produce wine.

JOEL'S T.O.T.C. BURGER

Difficulty: 🍷🍷
Prep Time: 45 minutes
Yield: 4 servings

Patties:
6 rashers bacon from the butcher
1/2 pound ground Italian sausage
1 1/2 pound lean ground chuck
1/4 cup Zinfandel
1/4 cup Manwich Sloppy Joe Sauce©
1 teaspoon Worcestershire Sauce
3 cloves fresh garlic, minced
Fresh ground pepper
Sea salt

Spread:
4 tablespoons mayonnaise
1 tablespoon Manwich Sauce
1 tablespoon sweet pickle relish

Garnish:
2 tomatoes, sliced
1 red onion, sliced
4 iceberg lettuce leaves
Salt and pepper, to taste

4 Fresh Rolls (Kaiser/Onion)

1. In an already hot saucepan, fry the thick slices of bacon until crisp. Drain the bacon. Crumble into small bits.

2. In large bowl, mix bacon, sausage, beef, Zinfandel, Manwich Sauce, Worcestershire Sauce, garlic, pepper, salt. Form into four patties.

3. Cook on grill 10-15 minutes each side (do not press on patties with spatula - it squeezes out the flavors!). Flame high to start, and then low to finish.

4. Make spread by mixing mayo, Manwich & relish.

5. Toast rolls on grill, Assemble burgers with garnish and spread (cheddar cheese optional). Serve with remaining Zinfandel.

This burger can be made year round. For February grilling, place towel on floor in front of outside door. Wear deck shoes or boots and use umbrella.

Contributed by artist Bob Johnson.

Would you be interested in a diet that claims to cut heart disease by 76% in men?

When the British Medical Journal ran a paper advocating the "Polypill" (combining aspirin, folic acid and cholesterol-lowering and blood-pressure drugs) for everybody over 55, some scientists devised a more natural alternative called the "Polymeal". The Polymeal advocates a diet of wine, dark chocolate, fish, fruits and vegetables, garlic and almonds to substantially reduce the risk of cardiovascular disease. A man can expect to live 6.6 years longer and a woman 4.8 years longer by simply eating the right meal once a day, according to study doctors.

The study suggested a person should daily consume 150 milliliters of red wine (about half a glass) and 100 grams of dark (bittersweet) chocolate.

While we don't recommend diets, the term "polymeal" is simply a new name for an old concept: using healing foods as medicine. To maximize health benefits, one should avoid smoking and combine the polymeal with exercise (*see Physical Activity suggestions on page 239*).

LAMB SHANKS OVER HERB POLENTA

Difficulty: ❢ ❢ ❢
Preparation Time: 2 hours
Yield: 6 servings

Shanks:
6 large lamb shanks (20 ounces)
Kosher salt and black pepper
4 tablespoons extra virgin olive oil
1 red onion, diced
1/2 cup whole, peeled garlic cloves
4 sprigs fresh rosemary (6-inches)
1/2 cup oil-cured olives
2 pounds fresh baby artichokes
2 cups Zinfandel
1 cup chopped tomatoes
2 cups veal stock

Polenta:
1 cup polenta
4 cups chicken stock
1 tablespoon chopped fresh garlic
2 tablespoons chopped fresh parsley
1 teaspoon kosher salt
1/2 teaspoon black pepper
1/2 cup grated dry jack cheese

1. Trim off tough leaves from artichokes and snip off the tops and bottoms of any rough edges. Set aside.

2. Liberally salt and pepper the shanks. In a heavy bottom pot, brown shanks in olive oil. Remove and set aside.

3. Add the onion and garlic to the pot and sauté. Add tomatoes, wine, stock and the shanks. Bring to a boil, then simmer, covered, for 1 hour.

4. Add olives, artichokes and rosemary. Cover and cook until meat and artichokes are tender, approximately 1 hour. Keep warm.

5. For polenta, bring stock, garlic, salt and pepper to a boil. Whisk in polenta and let simmer for 15 minutes, whisking occasionally.

6. Add parsley and cheese when polenta is soft. Remove from heat. Serve shanks with polenta. Garnish with more fresh rosemary.

Contributed by Chef Robin Lehnhoff of Lake Sonoma Winery

I n red wine, the tannins are responsible for the dark red or blue stains on your teeth, lips and tongue. The tannins also act as a natural preservative, allowing wine to age. Grape varieties differ in the amount of tannins in their skins, and the longer the juice is in contact with the skins during fermentation, the greater the tannins that will result in the wine. White wine is made by removing the juice from the skin, which is why tannins are absent from these wines. So after enjoying a firm red (one with many tannins), simply smile and allow your purple lips, tongue and teeth to share how fantastic it really was.

LISA'S PASTA SAUCE

Difficulty: ♟♟
Preparation Time: 4 to 8 hours
Yield: 6 servings

Crockpot meat sauce:
1 pound ground chuck
1/2 pound Italian sausage
28 ounce can Italian tomatoes with basil
6 ounce can tomato paste
1 medium onion, finely chopped
1/4 cup dry red wine
2 tablespoons parsley, chopped
1 teaspoon sugar
1 teaspoon dried basil leaves
1 teaspoon salt
1/4 teaspoon garlic powder
1/8 teaspoon pepper

1. Remove Italian sausage from casings and place in a large skillet. Brown ground chuck and Italian sausage with chopped onion until crumbly. Drain accumulated fat. Set aside to combine in Crockpot after adding other ingredients.

2. Add can of Italian tomatoes to Crockpot. If desired, use a hand-held blender and break up tomatoes to a finer consistency.

3. Add the rest of the ingredients, including meat mixture, to Crockpot. Stir to blend.

4. Cover and cook on high for 3 1/2 to 4 hours or on low for 7 to 8 hours.

5. Serve over your favorite pasta.

LOBSTER NAPOLEON WITH VANILLA SAUCE AND MANGO SALSA

Difficulty: ♟♟♟
Preparation Time: 40 minutes
Yield: 6-8 servings

1 package puff pastry
12-14 ounces lobster meat, cooked
1/4 of a vanilla bean
1 cup Brut
1 cup heavy cream
1 tablespoon unsalted butter
1 tablespoon fresh chives, minced
Salt and pepper, to taste

Mango Salsa:
1/2 cup fresh mango, diced
1 teaspoon fresh ginger root, minced
1 teaspoon rice wine vinegar
1 teaspoon salad oil
1 teaspoon fresh mint, minced
1/2 teaspoon jalapeño, minced
1/2 tablespoon fresh red onion, minced

1. Heat oven to 400°.

2. Cut puff pastry into 3 to 4-inch squares. Cut each square in half diagonally to form 2 triangles. Bake triangles for 8-12 minutes or until golden brown.

3. Meanwhile, for salsa, combine all ingredients and toss gently to mix thoroughly. Keep chilled until ready to serve.

4. When pastry is cool, cut each triangle in half to form a bottom and top. Set aside.

5. Combine wine with vanilla bean in medium saucepan and gently simmer over low heat until wine is reduced by two-thirds. Add heavy cream and continue to simmer until cream is reduced by one-half.

6. Add lobster meat and gently toss to evenly coat and warm lobster. Add butter and chives. Season to taste with salt and pepper.

7. To assemble, place lobster between two pastry triangles. Drizzle salsa around napoleon and serve.

Contributed by Thornton Winery

MOROCCAN LAMB OVER COUSCOUS

Cabernet Sauvignon adds wonderful flavor to the lamb in this dish.

Difficulty: ❦❦❦❦
Preparation Time: 2 hours plus marinating time
Yield: 8 servings

2 pounds fresh lamb stew meat
Extra virgin olive oil
1 large onion, sliced
2 cups chopped tomatoes
2 cups Cabernet Sauvignon
2 cups veal or lamb stock
Kosher salt and pepper
1/2 cup gold raisins
1/2 cup sliced Spanish olives
2 tablespoons fresh oregano
Couscous or rice

Moroccan Rub:
1 tablespoon fresh garlic, chopped
2 tablespoons extra virgin olive oil
1 1/2 teaspoons ground cumin
1 teaspoon ground ginger
1 teaspoon kosher salt
1/2 teaspoon tumeric
1/2 teaspoon paprika
1/4 teaspoon ground cinnamon
1/4 teaspoon ground black pepper

1. Combine all Moroccan rub ingredients in food processor and mix until you have a smooth paste. Cover lamb with rub. Let marinate for one day.

2. Heat oven to 350°.

3. In large sauté pan, sear lamb in olive oil and place in heavy-bottom roasting pan. Sauté onion, then add stock and tomatoes. Season with salt and pepper.

4. De-glaze pan with wine and pour mixture over lamb. Cover with foil and bake for 1 hour, just until meat is tender.

5. Add olives, raisins and oregano and cook for 30 minutes longer. Serve over couscous or rice.

Contributed by Chef Robin Lehnhoff of Kenwood Vineyards

WINE WORDS

Part One *"Tasting", Continued from Page 110*

♟ *Soft* – Soft wines bear no harshness on the palate and offer up mild tannins and acidity.

♟ *Spicy* – Cloves, mint, cinnamon, pepper and many more aromas call for a wine to be described as spicy.

♟ *Sweet* – More than fruity, this pertains to sugar levels in wine. However, even some "dry" wines will omit aromas of sweetness because of their intense fruit concentration.

♟ *Tart* – An indicator of acidic taste from the grape acids. In excess, this can be a negative.

♟ *Thin* – Wines that lack fullness and depth and seem watery are referred to as thin

♟ *Vinegary* – Easily caught by your nose or palate are those wines that produce a sharp sensation of spoiled wine.

♟ *Woody* – This is a negative term for wines that exude a smell of tainted or moldy oak from a barrel in poor condition or an overuse of new oak barrels.

MUSHROOM PEPPER STUFFED BEEF TENDERLOIN

Difficulty: ❦❦❦❦

Preparation Time: 1 hour

Yield: 8 servings

Mushroom Pepper Stuffing:

1 cup red bell pepper, chopped

4 tablespoons shallots, minced

5 tablespoons butter

2 tablespoons garlic, minced

1/4 pound shitake mushrooms

1/4 teaspoon salt

1/4 cup Merlot

Tenderloin:

3-4 pound beef tenderloin

Olive oil

Salt and freshly cracked pepper

Red Bell Pepper Sauce:

1 1/2 cups red bell pepper, chopped

7 tablespoons beef broth

1/4 teaspoon salt

2 teaspoons fresh lemon juice

8 tablespoons butter

2 tablespoons sour cream

1. For stuffing, sauté red bell pepper and shallots in butter until tender. Add garlic, mushrooms, salt and merlot. Sauté mixture until mushrooms are tender and liquid has evaporated. Remove from heat.

2. Slice tenderloin in half lengthwise yielding two pieces of meat approximately 8-inches long. Take a sharp knife, 8- to 9-inches long with a 1 1/4-inch blade ending in a point, and create a pocket approximately 1-inch in width inside the length of each piece of tenderloin. Do this by inserting the knife in one end of each piece of tenderloin and forcing the knife point almost to the other end, approximately 7-inches. Rotate the knife blade several times to create the pocket.

162

3. Stuff the pockets loosely with the mushroom pepper mixture and close the openings with a skewer to prevent the stuffing from coming out on the grill.

4. Brush the tenderloin with olive oil, salt and pepper.

5. Grill on open fire (or roast in oven at 400°) for 30-35 minutes for medium rare.

6. Meanwhile, for sauce, sauté red bell pepper in 4 tablespoons beef broth until all liquid is evaporated and peppers are tender.

7. Place mixture in food processor with remaining broth, salt and lemon juice. Purée.

8. Transfer mixture to sauté pan over medium heat. Add butter bit by bit until all is melted and well-blended. Whisk in sour cream until blended.

9. Slice cooked tenderloin into 1 1/2-inch thick portions and serve topped with sauce.

Contributed by Susan Auler of Fall Creek Vineyards

MUSTARD-CURED GRAVLAX, YUKON POTATO PANCAKE AND CARAWAY BLACK MUSTARD SEED CRÈME FRAICHE WITH MUSTARD "PAINT"

Winning recipe: 2006 Mustard Festival Critics Choice

Difficulty: ❦❦❦❦❦

Preparation Time: 11/2 hours plus standing/chilling time

Yield: 6 servings

Gravlax:

1 2-3 pound fresh salmon fillet (preferably center piece, skin on)
1 cup salt
1 cup sugar
2 tablespoons cracked black peppercorns
3 tablespoons mustard seed (toasted)
3 tablespoons Chardonnay

1. Mix salt, sugar, and black peppercorns.

2. Take a handful and rub it on both sides of the salmon. Place the salmon in a dish, and sprinkle the rest of the mix on top.

3. Sprinkle with Chardonnay, and let it stand for 6 hours at room temperature. Refrigerate for 24-30 hours, depending on how thick the salmon is.

Potato Pancake:

1 medium onion, cut into 1/4-inch dice
2 Russet (baking) potatoes (about 1 pound total)
1 large egg, lightly beaten
1/4 teaspoon black pepper
3/4 teaspoon salt
1 cup fine dry bread crumbs
1/2 cup vegetable oil, for frying

1. Peel potatoes and shred using large holes of a box grater. Squeeze potatoes by handfuls to eliminate excess moisture, then add egg, pepper, and salt, stirring until combined.

2. Spread 1/2 cup bread crumbs on a sheet of wax paper. Using a scant 1/4 cup potato mixture for each pancake, make 12 mounds on crumbs. Coat mounds with remaining 1/2 cup crumbs and flatten into 3-inch patties.

3. Heat oil in a 12-inch heavy skillet over moderate heat until hot but not smoking. Using a slotted spatula, gently shake off excess crumbs from each potato pancake, then fry in 2 batches, turning over once, until golden, about 6 minutes per batch. Transfer to paper towels to drain.

Caraway Black Mustard Seed Crème Fraiche:
1 cup crème fraiche
1 tablespoon caraway seed, toasted and ground in spice grinder
1 tablespoon black mustard seed
1/2 tablespoon chopped parsley

Mix ingredients, refrigerate at least 1 hour ahead.

Mustard "Paint":
1/2 cup dry mustard
3 tablespoons sugar
1/4 cup rice wine vinegar
4 tablespoons water
1/2 tablespoon turmeric
1 tablespoon wasabi powder

Mix ingredients, let stand 24 hours

3 ounces micro-mustard greens
1 ounce red tobiko caviar

To serve, "paint" plate with mustard. Place pancake on plate, mound with micro-mustard greens. Top with "rosette" of Gravlax, drizzle with crème fraiche and garnish with red tobiko caviar.

Contributed by Chef Maynard Oestreich of Artesa Vineyards & Winery

OSSO BUCCO ALLA MILANESE

Difficulty: ♟♟♟
Preparation Time:2 to 2 1/2 hours
Yield: 8 to 10 Servings

For Stew:
8 to 10 meaty cross-cut veal shanks
1/2 cup all-purpose flour
2 tablespoons olive oil
3 tablespoons unsalted butter
2 medium onions, halved lengthwise and thinly sliced
1 small carrot, finely chopped
1 celery rib, finely chopped
2 garlic cloves, finely chopped
1 cup dry white wine
1 cup chicken broth
1 28-32 ounce can whole plum tomatoes with juice (not in purée),
　coarsely chopped
1 cup Kalamata or other brine-cured black olives, pitted and halved
1 1/2 teaspoons fresh thyme leaves
1 Turkish or 1/2 California bay leaf
1 teaspoon salt, or to taste
1/2 teaspoon black pepper, or to taste

For gremolata:
3 tablespoons chopped fresh Italian parsley
1 large garlic clove, minced
1 teaspoon finely grated fresh lemon zest

Make Stew:
1. Preheat oven to 325.°

2. Pat shanks dry and season the season the meat with salt and pepper
and dredge in the flour. Tap off excess flour.

3. Heat oil and 2 tablespoons butter in ovenproof pot over moderately
high heat until foam subsides, then brown shanks well on all sides in
two batches, 10 to 12 minutes per batch, transferring to a plate.

4. Reduce heat to moderate and add remaining tablespoon butter to pot
along with onions, carrot, celery and garlic and cook, stirring, until

onions are pale golden, about 5 minutes. Add remaining stew ingredients and bring to a boil, stirring.

5. Carefully pack shanks on top of vegetables: stand the shanks upright to retain the marrow in the bones. Cover the pot and braise shanks in middle of oven until very tender, about 2 to 2 1/2 hours. Discard bay leaf.

Make gremolata and serve osso bucco:

1. Combine all of the ingredients for the gremolata in a bowl and sprinkle over osso bucco. Serve immediately

Contributed by Executive Chef Richard Graham of Martin & Weyrich Winery and Villa Toscana

> " "There is a tavern in the town,
> And there my true love sits him down,
> And drinks his wine with laughter and with glee,
> And never, never thinks of me." ~Anonymous

When Henry II of England married France's Eleanor of Aquitaine in 1152, her dowry included the vineyards of Bordeaux and Gascony. The light red wine produced there became known as Claret in England. By 1350, Claret had become so popular in England that Bordeaux was shipping them more than one million cases a year.

PORK CHOPS SAN FRANCISCO STYLE

Difficulty: 🍷🍷
Preparation Time: 1 hour
Yield: 4 servings

4 pork chops, 1/2 to 3/4-inch thick
1 tablespoon oil
1 clove garlic, crushed

Sauce:
2 teaspoons oil
4 tablespoons dry Sherry
2 tablespoons soy sauce
2 tablespoons brown sugar
1/2 teaspoon crushed red pepper
2 teaspoons cornstarch
2 tablespoons water

1. Trim fat off of pork chops. Heat oil in skillet and brown chops on both sides. Remove to a platter.

2. Add garlic to pan and sauté for one minute, being careful not to burn it.

3. For sauce, combine oil, Sherry, soy sauce, brown sugar and red pepper in a bowl. Mix well.

4. Return chops to skillet. Pour sauce over the top and cover tightly. Simmer over low heat until chops are tender and cooked through, approximately 35 minutes, turning once. If needed, add water to keep sauce from cooking down too low.

5. Remove chops from pan and keep warm. Dissolve cornstarch in water, add to sauce in pan and cook until thickened.

6. Serve chops over egg noodles, thin spaghetti, or rice with sauce poured over the top.

PORK FILET MIGNON WITH PORT WINE SAUCE

This dish pairs well with chive mashed potatoes and braised Swiss chard.

Difficulty: ♟♟♟
Preparation Time: 25 minutes
Yield: 4 servings

2 small pork tenderloins, sliced into 2-inch filets
1 tablespoon fresh sage, minced
1 tablespoon fresh rosemary, minced
2 tablespoons butter
Salt and freshly cracked pepper
1/2 cup shallots, minced
2 garlic cloves, minced
1 cup Port

1. Season filets with salt and pepper to taste. Sprinkle sage and rosemary on both sides and gently pat to attach them to the filets.

2. Melt 1 tablespoon of butter in a large, heavy sauté pan over medium-high heat. Add filets, a few at a time, and brown each on both sides until they are medium-rare. Remove to a platter and cover them with a bowl which seals to that platter. This allows them to continue cooking while relaxing the meat, which adds to its tenderness. Continue to brown the rest of the filets in the same way.

3. After all filets are done and resting, add remaining butter to the pan. Add shallots and garlic and sauté until tender. Add the wine and reduce by one half.

4. Return meat to the pan and coat with the sauce on all sides. Transfer filets to serving plates and drizzle the sauce over the filets and chive mashed potatoes, if serving.

Contributed by Pedroncelli Winery and Vineyards

RED CHILI WITH DOLCETTO

Difficulty: ♟♟

Preparation Time: 1 1/2 hours

Yield: 8 servings

1 pound ground chuck
1 pound breakfast sausage
1 cup diced onions
3 tablespoons garlic, minced
2 ounces Dolcetto or Zinfandel
3 cups kidney beans
2 cups condensed tomato soup
2 tablespoons chili powder
1 tablespoon cumin
1 teaspoon cayenne pepper
1 tablespoon flour
4 ounces water
Salt and pepper, to taste

1. Brown the ground chuck and breakfast sausage in Dutch oven in 3 tablespoons of olive oil. Add and cook onions and garlic for 10 minutes. De-glaze the pan with Dolcetto wine. Add kidney beans and tomato soup. Make into a paste and blend in chili powder, cumin, cayenne pepper, flour and water.

2. Cook over low heat, stirring frequently for 45 minutes to 1 hour. Salt and pepper to taste.

Contributed by Chef Shawn Stanchfield of Bargetto Winery

ROAST FILET MIGNON WITH GORGONZOLA CHEESE, CARAMELIZED ONIONS AND CABERNET SYRUP

Difficulty: ♟♟♟
Preparation Time: 40 minutes plus marinating time
Yield: 6

1 whole filet mignon (completely clean of fat, silver skin and
  veil meat)
1/2 cup chopped garlic
4 bay leaves
1 yellow onion, sliced
1 cup olive oil
1/2 cup fresh herbs chopped
3 tablespoons freshly ground black pepper
1/2 pound Gorgonzola cheese
3 yellow onions cut into rings (1/2-inch)
1/2 bottle Cabernet
1/2 cup brown sugar
1 cup demi-glace
1/4 pound butter
3 tablespoons olive oil
Salt and black pepper, to taste

1. Combine filet mignon and following 7 ingredients and marinade for 12 hours.

2. Heat oven to 400°.

3. In a heavy bottom saucepan, reduce Cabernet, sugar and demi-glace reduce to a syrup consistency, then whisk in butter.

4. Pat filet down, and pan-sear all sides.

5. Place in oven for 13 minutes or to desired doneness. (internal temperature 125° for medium rare)

6. While filet is in the oven, heat 3 tablespoons olive oil in pan and sauté onions over medium heat until caramelized.

7. Slice filet into 1/2-inch medallion and garnish with onions, crumbled Gorgonzola cheese and drizzle with Cabernet syrup.

Contributed by Chef Maynard Oestreich of Artesa Vineyards & Winery

SAUVIGNON BLANC STEAMED MUSSELS

Difficulty: ♟♟♟

Preparation Time: 35 minutes

Yield: 4 servings

5 pounds fresh mussels

3 tablespoons olive oil

1 cup leek, thinly sliced

1 cup celery, thinly sliced

1 tablespoon ginger, finely chopped

1 tablespoon garlic, finely chopped

3 cups Sauvignon Blanc

1 cup water

1 teaspoon coriander seed, crushed

1/4 cup pitted green olives, finely chopped

1 tablespoon capers, coarsely chopped

1 bunch flat leaf parsley, chopped

1 tablespoon lemon juice

3 tablespoons butter

Sea salt & white pepper

1. Wash mussels thoroughly, discarding any broken shells or dead mussels.

2. Over medium-high heat in large pot or steamer, add olive oil, leeks, celery, garlic and coriander seed. Sauté for 2 minutes. Increase the heat to high adding mussels, water and wine. Cover and steam for approximately 5 minutes or until shells open.

3. Scoop out mussels into serving bowls and reduce cooking liquid by half. Add remaining ingredients, whisking in butter at the end. Season to taste and pour over cooked mussels. Serve plenty of crusty bread along side to soak up the delicious broth.

Contributed by Mission Hill Family Estate

SHRIMP SCAMPI

Difficulty: 🍷🍷
Preparation Time: 20 minutes
Yield: 4 servings

1/2 cup butter
3 cloves garlic, crushed
2 tablespoons olive oil
24 large or jumbo shrimp, peeled and deveined
2 tablespoons parsley
1/3 cup dry white wine
1 tablespoon lemon juice
Salt and pepper to taste

1. Heat butter, garlic and olive oil in large skillet. Add shrimp and sauté on both sides until done, about 6 minutes. Remove shrimp to platter and keep warm.

2. Add remaining ingredients to pan. Cook on high for 1 minute. Pour sauce over shrimp and serve over cooked rice.

*"May you get all your wishes but one,
so you always have something to strive for!"*
– Unknown

SICILIAN BEEFSTEAK

Difficulty: ♟♟

Preparation Time: 30 minutes

Yield: 6 servings

1/2 cup olive oil
3 garlic cloves, crushed
6 beef steaks, 1/3 pound each
8 large tomatoes, peeled and chopped
3/4 cup black olives, pitted and sliced
2/3 cup sweet peppers, sliced
1 cup celery, diced
1/4 cup Cabernet Sauvignon or Chianti
3 tablespoons capers
Salt and pepper to taste
1 teaspoon oregano

1. In a large skillet, heat oil and sauté garlic until brown. Remove and set aside. Brown steaks in the pan (as many at a time the pan size allows) until desired doneness, approximately 6 minutes each side. Keep warm on a platter.

2. In the skillet, place olives, peppers, celery, tomatoes, capers, wine, salt and pepper. Sprinkle with oregano. Return steaks and garlic to pan. Cook gently for about 10 minutes. Serve steaks with vegetable sauce over each.

Fiasco (plural- fiaschi) is the Italian word for "flask". The word is often used to describe the round-bottomed, straw-covered bottle containing Chianti. The straw covering helps the bottle sit upright and protects the fragile glass bottle from breaking. Since cheaper wines come in these bottles, fiaschi are becoming less common as the cost of hand-wrapping each flask has become prohibitive.

SOLE FILETS IN WHITE WINE SAUCE

Difficulty: ♟♟
Preparation Time: 30 minutes
Yield: 6 servings

6 sole filets
1 cup water or fish stock
Salt and pepper
6 tablespoons butter, divided
One bunch of green onions, chopped
1/2 cup dry white wine
1 tablespoon flour
1/2 cup cream

1. Halve filets lengthwise, roll up each half and secure with toothpicks. Melt 3 tablespoons of butter in skillet. Add water or fish stock, salt and pepper to taste, green onions, wine and rolled filets. Bring to a boil, reduce heat and simmer on low until fish is white in the center, about 15 minutes. Remove to a platter and keep warm.

2. Reduce pan liquid to one third. Blend flour with cream and add to pan. Add remaining butter. Heat, stirring constantly, until smooth. Strain and pour over platter of fish.

SPICY SHRIMP FETTUCCINE

Difficulty: ♟♟

Preparation Time: 35 minutes

Yield: 8 servings

1 1/4 pounds dry fettuccine pasta
1/4 cup butter
11/4 pounds shrimp, peeled and deveined
2/3 cup Pinot Gris
2 tablespoons and 2 teaspoons lime juice
2/3 bunch cilantro, finely chopped
1/8 teaspoon cayenne pepper
Salt and pepper, to taste

1. Bring a large pot of water to boil, add fettuccine noodles and return water to boil. Cook until noodles are al dente. Drain well.

2. Meanwhile, in a large skillet, melt butter over medium heat, add shrimp and cook about 3 minutes, until shrimp turn pink. Remove shrimp from heat and set aside.

3. Pour wine and lime juice into the skillet used to cook the shrimp. Bring the mixture to a boil. Boil until the mixture is reduced by half, about 2 minutes.

4. Return shrimp to skillet. Add cilantro, cayenne pepper and salt and pepper. Stir to heat the mixture through, about 2 minutes.

5. Toss with pasta and serve.

Contributed by Callaway Vineyard and Winery

SUN-DRIED TOMATO AND PROSCIUTTO STUFFED CHICKEN BREASTS

Difficulty: ❦❦❦❦
Preparation Time: 50 minutes
Yield: 4 servings

Four 8-ounce boneless, skinless chicken breasts
4 thin slices prosciutto
4 slices white cheese
1 teaspoon fresh basil

Sun-Dried Tomato Sauce:
1 tablespoon olive oil
1 shallot, minced
1/4 cup sun-dried tomatoes in oil, minced
1 clove garlic, minced
Salt and pepper to taste
1/4 cup roma tomatoes, finely chopped
2 tablespoons Blanco Grande or other dry white wine
2 tablespoons chicken stock
1 tablespoon fresh basil, finely chopped
3 tablespoons heavy cream
2 tablespoons orange juice
1 tablespoon unsalted butter

1. Heat oven to 350°.

2. For sauce, sauté the shallots, sun-dried tomatoes and garlic in olive oil for 2 minutes. Add tomatoes, wine, chicken stock and basil. Reduce by two thirds.

3. Add heavy cream and simmer. Add orange juice and season with salt and pepper to taste. Finish the sauce by swirling in butter until melted.

4. Place each breast between plastic wrap and flatten with a rolling pin or meat mallet.

5. Spread one half of each breast with sauce. Place prosciutto and cheese slices on top of sauce. Sprinkle with basil. Fold over other half of breast and form a roll.

6. Secure with kitchen twine and bake for 25 to 30 minutes.

Contributed by Chef Dana Taylor of Los Pinos Ranch Vineyards

SWORDFISH STEAKS WITH CHARDONNAY SAUCE

Difficulty: 🍷🍷
Preparation Time: 30 minutes
Yield: 4 servings

4 swordfish steaks
Salt and pepper
1 tablespoon extra virgin olive oil
1/2 cup Chardonnay
2 large tomatoes, chopped
1 bunch chives, chopped
1 clove garlic, chopped
3 tarragon sprigs, chopped
2 tablespoons butter, cut into 4 smaller squares
Juice from 1/2 lemon
Chives for garnish

1. Season swordfish steaks on both sides with salt and pepper. Heat oil in large non-stick pan over medium heat. Add fish and sauté until browned, 2 to 4 minutes on each side. Transfer steaks to platter and keep warm.

2. Add Chardonnay to pan. Simmer 1 minute. Stir in tomatoes, chives, garlic and tarragon and stir 1 minute. Remove pan from heat and add butter until it softens and thickens the sauce slightly. Add a squeeze of lemon. Adjust seasonings to taste.

3. Spoon sauce over swordfish steaks and garnish with chives.

Contributed by Gnekow Family Winery

THYME-BRAISED PORK LOIN

Difficulty: ♟♟♟♟
Preparation Time: 3 1/2 hours
Yield: 8 servings

3 tablespoons unsalted butter
10 garlic cloves, minced
2 medium onions, finely chopped
2 carrots, finely chopped
2 celery ribs, finely chopped
Sea salt
Fresh ground black pepper
5-pound untrimmed pork loin
2 teaspoons thyme leaves
2 bunches thyme sprigs
1/4 cup extra virgin olive oil
2-3 cups Collina Bianca or another dry white wine

1. Heat oven to 300°.

2. Melt butter on stove in large, non-reactive roasting pan. Add garlic and onions and season with salt and pepper to taste. Cook over medium heat, stirring constantly, until softened, about 5 minutes.

3. Season pork loin on all sides with salt, pepper and thyme leaves. Sear pork in olive oil in pan over moderate heat until browned on all sides. Transfer all to a platter.

4. Drain pan and then wipe clean. Place carrots, celery, garlic and onions in the bottom of pan. Place pork on top of vegetables. Add wine, oil and thyme sprigs and bring to a boil.

5. Transfer pan to oven, cover and braise for about 2 1/2 hours, or until pork is very tender, basting every 30 minutes. Uncover for last 1/2 hour to allow juices to concentrate.

6. Place pork on carving board and season with salt and pepper to taste, loosely cover with aluminum foil and let stand for about 15 minutes.

7. Strain the pan juices through a fine sieve and use for gravy.

8. To serve, thickly slice pork and serve with the juices.

Contributed by Chef Russell Kane of Pleasant Hill Winery

TORTILLA-ENCRUSTED HALIBUT WITH CHARDONNAY

Difficulty: 🍷🍷🍷
Preparation Time: 30 minutes
Yield: 4 servings

1 16-ounce bag tortilla chips, restaurant style
4 halibut boneless fillets (5 to 6 ounces each)
8 ounces low sodium canned chicken stock
2 ounces Chardonnay
2 ounces canola oil
2 ounces butter
1/2 lemon
2 tablespoons cornstarch
Salt and white pepper, to taste

1. Heat oven to 350°.

2. Put tortilla chips in a large bowl and mash until coarsely ground. Set aside. Salt and pepper boneless halibut fillets. Heat sauté pan and add canola oil.

3. Dredge halibut in the tortilla chips. Note: they won't stick that well so you will need to spend a minute or two positioning the chips on the halibut.

4. Carefully add to the hot pan. Do not move the halibut in the pan. If you do, the tortilla chips will fall off. Once they are golden brown, turn over and brown the other side. Remove them from heat and finish in the oven until fish flakes easily.

Sauce:
1. Add Chardonnay in the pan (over heat) to de-glaze. Add lemon and chicken stock and reduce by half. Add cornstarch* to thicken. Finish by swirling butter into the sauce. Add salt and pepper to taste (white pepper). Strain and serve.

*Note: When thickening with cornstarch, you first add the cornstarch to cold water and mix together. When thickening, the cornstarch can only be added to a boiling liquid. Add small amounts until you reach the desired consistency. The desired thickness should coat the back of a spoon.

Contributed by Chef Shawn Stanchfield of Bargetto Winery

VEAL SAMBROSA

Difficulty: ♟♟
Preparation Time: 45 minutes
Yield: 6 servings

1/4 cup flour
1/2 cup Parmesan cheese
1 teaspoon salt
1/4 teaspoon pepper
1 1/2 pounds veal cutlets, sliced into 2-inch cubes
2 tablespoons olive oil
1 clove garlic, quartered
3/4 cup dry white wine
1/2 cup consommé
1 tablespoon lemon juice
Chopped parsley

1. Wipe the meat dry. Mix flour, cheese, salt and pepper together. Sprinkle the meat with flour mixture and pound it into the cubes.

2. Heat olive oil with garlic and brown the meat in it lightly on all sides. Remove garlic and add wine, consommé and lemon juice. Cover and simmer slowly for about 30 minutes. Remove to a platter and garnish with parsley.

VINTNERS STEW

Difficulty: ♟
Preparation Time: 6 hours
Yield: 8 servings

4 pounds beef stew meat, unbrowned, uncooked, in chunks
3 to 4 potatoes, cut into bite-size chunks
3 to 4 carrots, cut into bite-size chunks
3 to 4 ribs celery, cut into bite-size chunks
1 large onion, chopped
1 green bell pepper, chopped
1 clove garlic, crushed
1 can tomato soup
1 beef boullion cube
1 cup Cabernet Sauvignon
16-ounce can chopped tomatoes
1 tablespoon A-1® sauce
4 tablespoons Minute® tapioca
Salt and pepper, to taste

1. Heat oven to 275°.

2. Cut all vegetables into chunks.

3. Place all ingredients in a heavy kettle and bake, covered, for
5 hours. Add additional water or wine, if necessary, during cooking.
Stir during the last hour of baking.

Contributed by Callaway Vineyard and Winery

WILD DUCK ZINFANDEL

Difficulty: ❚❚❚❚
Preparation Time: 3 hours and 20 minutes
Yield: 6-8 servings

3 ducks
Salt and pepper to taste
6 celery stalks
1 1/2 quarts seasoned bread stuffing
1 1/2 cloves garlic
1/2 cup water
1 cup Zinfandel
1/4 cup orange marmalade
1/4 cup currant jelly
1 orange, diced, including rind
1/2 lemon diced, including rind
1 tablespoon browning sauce
2 quarts chicken broth
Flour
Dash of tarragon

1. Heat oven to 450°.

2. Season ducks with salt and pepper to taste. Place 2 celery stalks in each cavity. Bake ducks, breast sides up, for 30 minutes or until golden brown.

3. Remove from oven and reduce temp to 400°. Remove celery and drain ducks, discarding drippings.

4. Fill each duck with 1/2 quart stuffing and 1/2 garlic clove. Place breast sides down in roasting pan. Add 1/2 cup water and next 7 ingredients. Add extra broth if necessary for broth to almost cover ducks. Cover pan loosely with aluminum foil and bake for 2 1/2 hours or until tender.

5. Remove ducks from pan and skim off fat from gravy. Add tarragon to gravy and bring to boil. Cook until reduced by one half. Thicken with flour and strain. Serve ducks with gravy and wild rice.

Contributed by Gnekow Family Winery

wine wit

WINE COUNTRY CASSOULET

The sausage flavors in this dish can be varied. When using unsmoked sausages, however, be sure to precook them prior to sauteing with the other ingredients.

Difficulty: ♥♥♥♥
Preparation Time: 2 hours plus soaking time
Yield: 12 servings

2 tablespoons olive oil
1 pound andouille sausage, sliced
1 pound smoked chicken sausage, sliced
1 pound whiskey fennel sausage, sliced
1 large roasting chicken, cooked, picked and diced
4 large leeks, sliced
2 tablespoons chopped fresh garlic
1 large tart apple, peeled and chopped
2 teaspoons dry rubbed sage
1 tablespoons chopped fresh rosemary
2 bay leaves
1 cup Syrah
4 cups diced canned tomatoes
1 pound dry white beans, presoaked overnight
1 pound flageolet, presoaked overnight
2-3 cups chicken stock
1/2 cup tomato paste
1/2 teaspoon ground cloves
1/2 teaspoon ground mace
Salt and pepper to taste
4 tablespoons olive oil
4 cups Panko bread crumbs
1/2 cup chopped fresh parsley

1. Heat oven to 350°.

2. Sauté sausages in olive oil until browned. Remove from pan and set aside.

3. Sauté garlic and leeks until soft. Add apple, herbs and chicken meat. Add wine and cook down. Add tomatoes, beans, tomato paste, spices, chicken stock and sautéed sausages. Season with salt and pepper. Pour into Dutch oven or large, heavy casserole. Liquid should almost cover

beans and sausages. Add more stock or water if necessary.

4. Toss Panko with olive oil and parsley. Season with salt and pepper. Sprinkle over cassoulet and cover. Bake for 1 1/2 hours or until beans are tender. Remove foil or lid and brown top for 10 minutes before serving.

Contributed by Chef Robin Lehnhoff of Valley of the Moon Winery

Fine wine storage options:

1 A wine fridge, or wine cave, is a refrigerator made for storing wine. Wine fridges range in size from small countertop models that hold 10 or fewer bottles to very large sizes that can hold more than 500 bottles.

2 A wine cellar can be your basement or another lightly used room in your home. You can buy or have a professionally designed cellar installed. A less expensive option is to simply install a cooling unit (specialized air conditioner) in the basement or room you intend to use.

3 A wine closet is the least expensive option. If you live in a climate with moderate temperatures, you may choose to store the wine in one of your home closets.

4 Storage lockers at offsite locations are a good option if you don't have room to properly store the bottles at home. Local wine merchants may rent storage space or wine lockers to individuals for storing their private collections.

DESSERTS

BROWNIE SUNDAE WITH MERLOT FUDGE SAUCE

Difficulty: ♟
Preparation Time: 1 hour
Yield: 6 servings

2 pints coffee ice cream, or your favorite flavor
1 jar Chocolate Hazelnut Merlot Fudge, softened in the microwave
3 Skor bars, roughly chopped
1/2 cup hazelnuts, toasted, skins removed and roughly chopped
Brownies
Whipped cream

1. Prepare brownies according to instructions. Let cool. Cut into generous squares and then slice diagonally to form triangles.

2. In serving dish, place the brownie on the bottom. Top with a scoop of ice cream, chocolate sauce, a sprinkling of Skor bars and nuts. Repeat until you have two or three layers. Top with whipped cream and serve immediately.

Whipped Cream:
Heavy whipping cream
1 teaspoon vanilla extract
Powdered sugar

Immediately before serving, whip cream until semi-stiff peaks have formed. Add vanilla and enough sugar to lightly sweeten the whipped cream.

Contributed by Lambert Bridge Winery

CHAMPAGNE-LAVENDER CAKE

Difficulty: ♟♟♟

Preparation Time: 1 hour

Yield: 12 servings

2 3/4 cups all purpose flour
3 teaspoons baking powder
1 teaspoon salt
1 teaspoon lavender flowers, ground to dust
2/3 cup butter
1 1/2 cups granulated sugar
3/4 cup Sec Champagne
6 egg whites
Powdered sugar (optional)

1. Heat oven to 350°. Prepare 10-inch round cake pan with cooking spray or butter.

2. Sift flour, baking powder, salt and lavender. Set aside.

3. In another bowl, cream together butter and sugar until light and fluffy.

4. Alternately add flour mixture and Champagne to butter mixture.

5. Whip egg whites in clean, dry bowl until stiff peaks form. Fold half of the egg whites into batter, then the remaining until incorporated. Pour into prepared pan.

6. Bake cake 25 to 30 minutes. Cool and dust with powdered sugar if desired.

Contributed by Chef Robin Lehnhoff of Korbel Champagne Cellars

WINE WORDS

Part Two: *Words used in grape growing and winemaking:*

❦ *Appellation* – The geographical area where the grapes used to make a wine are grown.

❦ *Aging* – The time spent for a wine to mature and its flavors and aromas to develop. There is barrel aging ,with the wine in a cask between fermentation and bottling, and bottle aging.

❦ *Blend* – This is when a winemaker combines two or more grape varieties, vintages or locations to create a new wine with balance and quality.

❦ *Brix* – This is a measurement of the percentage of sugar content the grapes have just before they are harvested.

❦ *Cap* – As red wine sits fermenting, the cap is a thick cake of grape skins that floats on top.

❦ *Crush* – The process of turning grapes into a juice by separating out the seeds and skins. In days of yore, or *I Love Lucy* episodes, this was done by stomping the grapes with your feet in a barrel.

❦ *Enology or Oenology* – The science of winemaking.

❦ *Estate Bottled* – If labeled as such, 100% of the grapes have been grown on the land controlled by the winery in the same viticultural area and have been crushed, fermented, finished, aged and bottled by them.

❦ *Fermentation* – The process of turning grape sugars into alcohol and carbon dioxide by adding yeast. In other words, what turns grape juice into wine.

❦ *Continued on Page 206*

CHAUCER'S OLALLIEBERRY WINE CRÈME BRÛLÉE

Difficulty: 🍷🍷
Preparation Time: 2 hours
Yield: 8 servings

4 cups cream
1/2 cup Olallieberry wine
1 cup sugar
12 egg yolks

1. Heat oven to 275°.

2. Put cream and wine in a sauce pot and bring to a boil. Take egg yolks and sugar and whisk together in a bowl. Add hot cream to egg yolks while whisking a little at a time so you don't make scrambled eggs.

3. Once all the cream is in with the yolks, scoop off all the foam that is on the top. Pour into 8 small dishes that are oven safe. Put dishes on a sheet pan with sides. Add a small amount of hot water onto the sheet pan so the crème brulées don't burn on the bottom.

4. Bake in an oven for about 1 1/2 hours or until they jiggle like Jell-O®. To brûlée the top, sprinkle granulated sugar on the top of the crème brulée evenly and stick under the broiler in your oven until desired color (golden brown). Let cool for 5 minutes before serving.

Contributed by Beth Paiva, Pastry Chef of Bargetto Winery

CHERRY BROWNIES

Difficulty: ♟
Preparation Time: 1 hour
Yield: 12 servings

1 package of your favorite brownie mix
2 eggs
1/2 cup vegetable oil
3 ounce package of cherry flavored gelatin
3/4 cup pie cherries
1 cup Cabernet Sauvignon or Merlot

1. Heat oven to 325°. Spray a 9x13-inch pan with cooking spray.

2. In a bowl, combine all ingredients except cherries. Fill greased pan with this mixture and place pie cherries on top of the batter. Press cherries lightly into the batter.

3. Bake for 45 minutes. Do not overbake. Let brownies cool before cutting.

Contributed by Preston Premium Wines

*"May we have more and more friends,
and need them less and less."*
– Unknown

Buzz on the Vine

Tasty Lessons From A Wine Club

Perusing the wine aisles of the local grocery or wine store can be a frustrating, love-hate relationship. You love discovering new wines. However, you hate browsing shelves filled with countless bottles of wine you know nothing about. Joining a wine club could be the answer.

"From Pinot Noir to Sauvignon Blanc there are thousands of great wines out there," says Bruce Boring, founder of The California Wine Club. "The challenge is finding the right one!"

That is why Bruce, along with his wife Pam, started The California Wine Club in 1990. "We liked wine but the 'wall of wine' exhausted us and we hated wasting good money on bad wine. We just wanted to find a great bottle of wine for dinner — and share the discovery with our friends," he says. And that's exactly what they've been doing.

"Wine clubs can be a great venue for learning about wine. You can experience a variety of styles from nearly everywhere without the stress of choosing the best ones," Bruce explains. "Plus, joining a club can expose wine lovers to wines they would not typically have access to."

The first step to picking a wine club is being prepared with key questions — relevant to your personal tastes and knowledge level — that will help facilitate the decision. For example: Who selects the wines that are featured? Are the wines guaranteed? Will every wine come from a real-working winery? Is there a chance to reorder more of a favorite? Getting answers to questions like these will help consumers identify which club is the best one for them.

"There is a wine club for everyone," Bruce admits. "The key is finding the one that speaks to your heart and your palate."

CHOCOLATE AND CUVÉE DE LA LUNA CREMA

Difficulty: ♟♟♟

Preparation Time: 30 minutes plus chilling time

Yield: 12 biscuits

1 cup Cuvée de la Luna or other hearty red wine
1/2 cup granulated sugar
1/4 cup granulated sugar
12 ounces bittersweet chocolate
8 ounces unsweetened chocolate
8 egg yolks
1 1/4 cups milk
2 cups heavy cream
1 tablespoon unsalted butter

1. In a small saucepan, combine wine and 1/2 cup sugar. Bring to a boil and reduce down by two thirds. Set aside.

2. Place chocolate in a bowl and melt over hot water bath.

3. In another saucepan, bring milk, 1 cup of cream and 1/4 cup sugar to a scald. (Just before the milk boils, there will be bubbles around the edge of pot and a light film will form on top.) Remove from heat.

4. Add wine mixture and egg yolks to chocolate and then add scalded milk. Whisk in butter until melted and smooth.

5. Pour into individual ramekins or martini glasses. Chill until ready to serve.

6. Just before serving, whip remaining 1 cup cream. Top ramekins with cream.

Contributed by Chef Robin Lehnhoff of Valley of the Moon Winery

wine wit

WINE WISDOM

"A good party is where you enjoy good people, and they taste even better with Champagne."
~Wilson Mizner~

"Here's to wine, it accentuates the curves and negates the brakes."
~George H. Boynton, Sr.~

"Back of this wine is the vintner, and back through the years his skill, and back of it all are the vines in the sun and the rain and the Master's Will."
~Vintner's Ode~

"Bouquet is the soul of the wine, while an agreeable aroma unfailingly imparts a delicious sensation."
~Frona Eunice Wait~

"Wine seems to have the power of attracting friendship, warming and fusing hearts together."
~Athanasius~

"Pour it and they will come."
~Professor Steven Mutkoski~

". . . that nectareous, delicious, precious, heavenly, joyful and divine liquor called wine."
~Francois Rabelais~

"One of the oldest and surest roads to contentment lies through the conventional trinity of wine, woman and song."
~Rexford Guy Tugwell~

"Here's [to] our next joyous meeting – and, oh, when we meet, may our wine be as bright and our union as sweet!"
~Thomas Moore~

"Wine is something magic; you are following it through the year."
~Lamberto Frescobaldi~

CHOCOLATE BALLS

These make an excellent holiday gift idea as they can keep up to 4 weeks.

Difficulty: 🍷🍷
Preparation Time: 20 minutes plus standing time
Yield: 40 balls

6 ounces semi-sweet chocolate chips
2 1/2 cups vanilla wafers, finely crushed
1/3 cup sweet red wine
1/4 cup honey
2 cups walnuts, ground
Granulated sugar

1. Melt chocolate chips and honey in a saucepan over low heat. Remove from heat and add in the vanilla wafer crumbs, nuts and wine.

2. Shape mixture into 1-inch balls and roll each in sugar. Store in an airtight container for at least 5 days while the flavors blend.

Here's a dream come true: chocolate truffles filled with tantalizing wines. Various wineries and chocolatiers offer truffles filled with Cabernet Sauvignon, Chardonnay, Port and more. They deliver a creamy, rich and elegant taste you won't quickly forget. Some offer chocolate sauces and other chocolate delights blended with red, white and dessert wines. Shop online or in person for a truly luscious experience.

"Laughter is therapeutic . . . and so is wine and chocolate!"
- John Rudy

CHOCOLATE PECAN PIE

Difficulty: 🍷🍷
Preparation Time: 1 1/2 hours
Yield: 6 servings

1 cup sugar
1 cup light corn syrup
1/2 cup butter
1/4 cup sweet white wine
4 eggs, beaten
2 teaspoons vanilla extract
1/4 teaspoon salt
6 ounces semi-sweet chocolate chips
1 cup pecans
1 pie crust

1. Heat oven to 325°.

2. Combine sugar, corn syrup, butter and wine in saucepan. Stir constantly over medium heat until butter melts and sugar dissolves.

3. Beat together eggs, vanilla and salt. Slowly pour egg mixture into sugar mixture, whisking constantly.

4. Stir in chocolate chips and pecans. Pour mixture into pie crust.

5. Bake 50 to 55 minutes or until set and golden.

Contributed by Susan Auler of Fall Creek Vineyards

CORKBOARD

Wine is fat-free and contains no cholesterol. It has roughly the same number of calories as grape juice and is a low-carb treat! Six ounces of red wine has just 2.9 grams of carbohydrates while white wine has just 1.35 grams.

The lip of a red wine glass is sloped inward to capture the aromas of the wine and deliver them to your nose.

The very slow interaction of oxygen and wine produces the changes one notices in aging wine.

Vintage Port can take forty years to reach maturity.

Grape varieties do not determine how sweet or how dry the wine will be; the winemaker does.

The Pinot Noir grape has more clones (over 100 registered) than any other wine grape variety. To cultivate a particular grape variety, grafting is used.

During the growing season, the canopy of leaves at the top of the vine is often cut away to increase exposure to the sun for ripening. This is called pruning.

Eighty pounds of coal, eight gallons of gasoline, and 240 bottles of table wine all contain the same amount of energy – 1 million BTU's (British Thermal Units).

The tradition of offering hosts the initial taste from a bottle of wine sprung up out of necessity. In order to prove the wine free of poison and fit to drink, the host would take the first sip of wine.

The wine cask, the ubiquitous soft plastic wine bag-in-a-box, was invented by Thomas Angove of Australia in 1965.

CHOCOLATE RASPBERRY CABERNET CAKE

Difficulty: ♟
Preparation Time: 1 1/2 hours
Yield: 12 servings

1 box chocolate cake mix
4 eggs
3 ounces raspberry gelatin
3/4 cup Cabernet Sauvignon
3/4 cup oil
3/4 cup raspberries

1. Heat oven to 350°. Grease and flour a bundt pan.

2. Blend all ingredients except raspberries in mixing bowl. Mix on medium speed for 2 minutes. Pour into greased pan and place raspberries on top of batter.

3. Bake for 1 hour. Let cool and dust with powdered sugar before serving.

Contributed by Preston Premium Wines

Maine enacted the first statewide law prohibiting the manufacture and sale of liquor in 1851, and Kansas became the first entirely "dry" state, in 1880.

During Prohibition, a loophole in the law allowed each home to "make 200 gallons of non-intoxicating cider and fruit juice per year". This turned thousands of otherwise law-abiding citizens into home winemakers and bootleggers.

Prohibition contributed to the demise of more than 500 wineries that existed prior to prohibition. The National Repeal of Prohibition went into effect on December 5, 1933.

FRESH PEACH AND YOGURT SOUP WITH PINOT GRIGIO

Difficulty: 🍷🍷

Preparation Time: 40 minutes plus chilling time

Yield: 6 servings

2 pounds fresh peaches
12 ounces Pinot Grigio
2 ounces honey
1 ounce lemon juice
1/8 teaspoon cinnamon, ground
4 ounces plain yogurt, non-fat
1/2 tablespoon heavy cream
Pistachios, chopped finely (optional)

1. Remove the pit from the peaches and roughly chop them, leaving the peels on. In a bowl, mix peaches, Pinot Grigio, honey and lemon juice.

2. Heat and simmer mixture for 25 minutes. Remember to use a non-reactive pan; no aluminum or copper. After simmering, remove and purée the peach mixture in a blender. A tip when puréeing any hot mixture is to start the blender first then add the ingredients. Sometimes, people add the hot mixture to the blender, cover, then watch it explode all over the kitchen walls when the blender is turned on. We don't want that to happen here.

3. Once blended, strain and chill. Stir in the cinnamon, yogurt and heavy cream. Chill thoroughly and serve in chilled bowls, garnished with the chopped pistachio nuts.

Contributed by Chef Shawn Stanchfield of Bargetto Winery

GEORGE'S TANGERINE BUNDT CAKE

Difficulty: ♟♟
Preparation Time: 2 hours
Yield: 12 servings

Cake:
3 cups flour
1 teaspoon baking powder
1/4 teaspoon salt
2 1/2 cups sugar
1 cup butter, very soft
2 tablespoons tangerine zest
1 teaspoon vanilla extract
5 eggs
1/4 cup dry white wine
1 cup milk

Infusion:
3/4 cup sugar
3 tablespoons butter
1/4 cup tangerine juice
2 tablespoons rum

1. Heat oven to 350°. Grease and lightly flour a bundt pan.

2. In a large mixing bowl, combine 2 1/2 cups sugar, soft butter, tangerine zest, vanilla and eggs. Beat with a mixer on low for 1 minute, stirring constantly.

3. In a medium bowl, mix flour, baking powder and salt. Combine wine and milk in a separate bowl.

4. Turn the mixer up to medium and beat for 6 minutes while alternating adding the flour mixture then the milk mixture to the bowl. Scrape the bowl to blend in each addition.

5. Pour into the bundt pan. Place pan on a cookie sheet and bake for 1 hour 15 minutes or until toothpick inserted into the middle comes out clean.

6. About 10 minutes before cake is done, mix the infusion ingredients together in a small saucepan. Heat on medium until dissolved.

7. Remove cake from the oven and poke a long skewer into the cake at 1-inch spaces all around. Spoon the rum infusion into the holes. Cool for 20 minutes in the pan.

8. Invert the cake from the pan onto a platter and then cool completely on a wire rack.

CELLAR CHALLENGE

Dessert Wine: Here's to your sweet tooth!

1. Ice wines are made from frozen grapes. The juice from these grapes has an extremely high sugar concentration. What country is the largest producer of these wines?
    a.) Germany
    b.) Austria
    c.) Switzerland
    d.) Canada

2. What are dessert wines called in Australia?
    a.) Sweeties
    b.) Stickies
    c.) Smarties
    d.) Skinnies

3. Sherry is a fortified wine, and genuine Sherry is only produced in the southernmost section of which country?
    a.) Spain
    b.) Portugal
    c.) Brazil
    d.) Italy

4. Port can be separated into two main categories: Wood Port and Bottle Port. Can you identify the Wood Port?
    a.) Crusted Port
    b.) Vintage Port
    c.) White Port
    d.) Vintage Character Port

 Solutions on page 243

HONEY APPLE CRISP

Difficulty: ♟♟
Preparation Time: 1 hour
Yield: 8 servings

4-5 cups Granny Smith apples, peeled and thinly sliced
1/4 cup granulated sugar
1 tablespoon lemon juice
1/4 cup light white wine
1/2 cup honey
1 cup flour, sifted
1/2 cup brown sugar, firmly packed
1 teaspoon salt
1/2 cup butter, softened

1. Heat oven to 375°.

2. Spread out the apple slices in an un-greased, 8x8-inch baking dish. Sprinkle them with the granulated sugar. Top with lemon juice, wine and honey.

3. In a bowl, mix flour, brown sugar and salt. Cut in the butter to the dry ingredients until the mixture is crumbly.

4. Spread mixture over the apples. Bake until apples are tender and topping is golden brown, approximately 40 minutes.

"May the luck of the Irish
Lead to happiest heights,
And the highway you travel,
Be lined with green lights."
– Irish Toast

LATE HARVEST GEWURZTRAMINER CHEESE-CAKE

Difficulty: 🍷🍷
Preparation Time: 2 hours plus cooling time
Yield: 8 servings

Crust:
1/4 cup graham cracker crumbs
1/4 cup sugar
1 teaspoon cinnamon
2 ounces butter, melted

Filling:
2 1/2 pounds cream cheese
8 ounces sugar
2 ounces corn starch
4 ounces cream
11/4 cup Late Harvest Gewürztraminer
5 large eggs

Crust:
1. Heat oven to 325°.

2. Mix all ingredients together, and flatten the graham cracker mix into a 12-inch cake pan. Bake for 7 minutes, set aside.

Filling:
1. Beat cream cheese, sugar, and corn starch until smooth. Scrape down bowl and add cream and mix. Scrape down bowl and add Gewürztraminer and mix. Scrape down bowl and mix on medium for 30 seconds.

2. Pour into graham cracker crust and bake for 1 1/2 hours until it jiggles like Jell-O®. Let cool at room temperature for 1 hour, then put in fridge for at least 6 to 24 hours before serving.

Contributed by Beth Paiva, Pastry Chef of Bargetto Winery

WINE WORDS

Part Two *"Winemaking", Continued from Page 190*

❦ *Grand Cru* – In France, Cru is growth and thereby Grand Cru is Great Growth. It designates the best.

❦ *Hang Time* – This is simply the time that a grape cluster is on the vine.

❦ Late Harvest – Indicates that grapes were left on the vine past their   normal harvest time. Wines from these grapes result in a higher sugar concentration.

❦ *Maceration* – A wine making technique of fermenting uncrushed grapes under pressure, producing fresh, fruity wine.

❦ *Must* – Crushed grapes with stems removed, it is the pulpy mass at any stage between grape juice and wine.

❦ *Oxidation* – An over-exposure to oxygen can cause grapes, grape juice, or wine to deteriorate and taste flat. Often caused in bottled wines by a less-than-airtight cork.

❦ *Pressing* – An important step in making white wines where the juice of the grape is literally pressed out of its skin.

❦ *Reserve* – Don't be fooled by this one. It has no legal meaning so wineries can use this term to designate any special bottling that they choose.

❦ *Residual Sugar* – After fermentation is complete, this measure (usually given as a percentage) is of the sugar left in the wine.

❦ *Continued on Page 221*

MUSCAT BERRY LAYER CAKE

Difficulty: ♥♥♥
Preparation Time: 20 minutes plus chilling time
Yield: 8 servings

1 quart of fresh strawberries, stemmed and sliced thin
1 pint of fresh raspberries
1 package of prepared lady fingers (approximately 40 pieces)
1 quart of bakers cream
2 cups of Muscat Canelli
2 cups lemon custard
Fresh mint, for garnish

1. Lightly drizzle lady fingers with the Muscat Canelli and place them around the edge of a springform pan, standing up. Place eight more on the bottom of the pan in a star pattern.

2. Sprinkle half of the raspberries over the lady fingers in the bottom of the pan. Gently spread half of the whipped cream over the lady fingers and raspberries. Carefully spread the lemon custard evenly over the layer of whipped cream.

3. Toss sliced strawberries with 3 tablespoons of the Muscat Canelli. Layer the sliced strawberries over the custard evenly.

4. Spread the remaining whipped cream over the strawberries. Place eight ladyfinger cakes on the top of the cake, repeating the star pattern on the bottom of the pan.

5. Cover with plastic wrap and allow to chill for at least 4 hours before serving.

6. Gently invert cake onto a serving dish and remove springform pan. Garnish with the remaining raspberries and fresh mint.

Contributed by Chef Corey Morse of Husch Vineyards

POACHED PEARS WITH ICE CREAM

Difficulty: 🍷🍷
Preparation Time: 1 hour plus chilling time
Yield: 6 servings

6 Bosc pears, peeled
1 quart red wine
1/2 cup honey
1 cup Port
1 stick cinnamon
6 scoops vanilla ice cream
1 pound semisweet chocolate chips
1 cup heavy cream
Roasted, sliced almonds

1. Place peeled pears in a stock pot. Add wine, honey, Port and cinnamon stick. Simmer for 45 minutes or until pears are cooked. Remove from stove and place in a bowl to cool. Place bowl in refrigerator and chill overnight.

2. Before serving, melt chocolate chips and cream together in a double boiler. To serve, place one scoop of ice cream in each bowl, place cold pear on top and drizzle each with the hot chocolate sauce. Finish with roasted almonds on top.

Contributed by Chef Didier Poirier of 71 Palm Restaurant

SINFUL CHOCOLATE CAKE WITH SYRAH FUDGE SAUCE

Try using butterscotch chips instead of chocolate chips for a different and delicious flavor. The fudge or butterscotch sauce can also be served over ice cream.

Difficulty: 🍷🍷
Preparation Time: 1 hour plus cooling time
Yield: 10-12 servings

Cake:
1 box yellow cake mix
1 package instant chocolate pudding mix
1 small carton sour cream
16-ounce package chocolate chips

Syrah Fudge Sauce:
1/2 cup un-salted butter
1 2/3 cups powdered sugar
6 ounces semi-sweet chocolate chips
1/3 cup evaporated milk
1/4 teaspoon salt
1/8 cup Syrah

1. Heat oven to 350°. Grease and flour a bundt pan.

2. Prepare cake batter according to directions on box. Blend in pudding mix, sour cream and chocolate chips.

3. Bake for 39 to 43 minutes or until toothpick comes out clean. Cool cake completely and then turn out onto serving plate.

4. For sauce, melt butter and sugar in the top of a double boiler. Blend in the chocolate chips and milk. Cook for 15 to 20 minutes.

5. Add Syrah and cook for an additional 10 minutes. Pour warm sauce over bundt cake.

6. Refrigerate and serve.

Contributed by Firestone Vineyard

WHITE CHOCOLATE MOUSSE WITH STRAWBERRY WINE

Difficulty: 🍷🍷
Preparation Time: 20 minutes
Yield: 8 servings

6 ounces white chocolate
1/3 cup milk
2 large egg whites
Pinch of cream of tartar
1 cup whipping cream
1 tablespoon white rum, optional
8 small chocolate cups
Strawberry wine

1. Place chocolate and milk in double boiler. Melt over moderate heat while stirring to ensure chocolate is completely melted. Remove from heat and set aside to cool to room temperature.

2. Beat egg whites with cream of tartar until stiff. Gently fold whites into chocolate mixture. Fold in whipped cream and rum. Spoon into individual ramekins.

3. Fill chocolate cups with wine. Place cup in each chocolate mousse.

4. Additional options: Pour wine over vanilla ice cream and add shaved bittersweet chocolate bark. Enhance your favorite dessert (fresh fruit, cheeses, ice cream, banana flambé, apple strudel, and any chocolate dessert) with strawberry wine.

Contributed by Baldwin Vineyards

WINE CAKE WITH JAM AND CREAM

Difficulty: 🍷🍷🍷
Preparation Time: 45 minutes plus freezing time
Yield: 12 servings

6 cups whipping cream
1 cup sugar
Two 9-inch layers of white cake
3/4 cup Sauvignon Blanc or Riesling
1/2 cup raspberry jam
1/2 cup apricot jam
2 cups sliced almonds

1. Whip cream until soft peaks form. Slowly add sugar and continue beating until stiff peaks form.

2. Split each cake layer in half, making 4 layers. Place first cake layer on serving plate, making sure this platter can fit into your freezer. Sprinkle that layer with about 1/4 of the wine, then spread with raspberry jam and 1 cup whipped cream.

3. Add next layer. Sprinkle with wine, then spread with apricot jam and 1 cup whipped cream.

4. Add third layer. Sprinkle with wine, spread with 1 cup whipped cream and sprinkle with 1/2 cup almonds. Add last layer and repeat the last process.

5. Frost top and sides with remaining whipped cream and sprinkle top with remaining almonds. Freeze cake. (About 6 to 8 hours)

6. Once cream on top and sides is firm, cover with plastic wrap. Approximately 1/2 hour before serving, move to the refrigerator to soften. Cut into thin slices.

WINE CAKE WITH SHERRY FROSTING

Difficulty: 🍷🍷
Preparation Time: 1 hour
Yield: 12 servings

Cake:
1 package yellow cake mix
3/4 cup oil
3/4 cup Symphony wine or dry Sherry
4 eggs
1 package vanilla pudding
3/4 teaspoon nutmeg

Frosting:
1/2 cup butter
1 package powdered sugar
1/4 cup cream Sherry

1. Heat oven to 350°. Grease and flour a tube pan.

2. In a mixing bowl, blend cake mix, oil and wine. Add eggs one at a time, mixing well after each addition. Add vanilla pudding and nutmeg and beat 4 minutes at medium speed.

3. Bake for 45 minutes.

4. For frosting, cream butter, adding sugar gradually. Add Sherry and blend well. Spread over cooled cake and serve.

Contributed by Mary Ann Sebastiani Cuneo on behalf of Sylvia Sebastiani of Sebastiani Vineyards and Winery

WINE COOKIES

Vary the wine you use to give these cookies different tastes.

Difficulty: 🍷🍷
Preparation Time: 45 minutes
Yield: about 4 dozen

1 cup wine, red or white
3/4 cup sugar
3/4 cup oil
1 teaspoon anise seed
Rind of 1/2 orange or 1 teaspoon dried rind
2 teaspoons baking powder
1 egg
4 1/2 cups flour
Granulated sugar

1. Heat oven to 350°. Grease a large cookie sheet.

2. Mix first seven ingredients together then add flour and blend well. Knead on a board.

3. Take one piece of dough and make a roll that is 6-inches long and 1/2 to 3/4-inches thick. This will be one cookie. Make a loop with the dough and put one end through to form a pretzel shape. Repeat with remaining dough.

4. Sprinkle cookies with additional sugar. Let stand about 20 minutes to rise slightly, then bake on a greased cookie sheet for 20 minutes.

Contributed by Baywood Cellars

WINE JELLY

Difficulty: ❢
Preparation Time: 15 minutes plus cooling time
Yield: 8 servings

2 envelopes unflavored gelatin
1/4 cup cold water
1 cup boiling water
2/3 cup sugar
Pinch of salt
1/4 cup lemon juice
1/4 cup orange juice
2 cups sweet Sherry
Sour or whipped cream

1. Soak gelatin in cold water about 10 minutes. Add boiling water and stir well. Cool partially.

2. Add sugar, salt, lemon juice, orange juice and Sherry. Place into a mold or dish to chill and congeal. Serve in dessert dishes and garnish with a dollop of sour or whipped cream.

"To my friends:
Friends we are today,
And friends we'll always be –
For I am wise to you,
And you can see through me."
– Unknown

CORKBOARD

RUDY

🍇 Christopher Columbus brought Sherry on his voyage to the New World.

🍇 The 55 drafters of the U.S. Constitution celebrated their success with 54 bottles of Madeira, 60 bottles of claret, 8 bottles of whiskey, 22 bottles of Port, 8 bottles of hard cider, 12 beers and 7 bowls of alcohol punch large enough that "ducks could swim in them".

🍇 The U.S nation's first wine expert was President Thomas Jefferson, who was very partial to fine Bordeaux and Madeira. In 1801, he spent $3,000 of his $25,000 salary on French wine he personally selected. He also helped stock the cellars of the 1st five U.S. Presidents.

🍇 The most expensive bottle of wine ever sold was 1787 Chateau Lafitte claret that was engraved with the initials of Thomas Jefferson. Sold at auction by Christies of London, in December, 1985, the buyer paid £105,000 ($157,000 US) for the bottle. Eleven months later, the cork dried out, slipped into the bottle and spoiled the wine, making it the most expensive bottle of vinegar!

🍇 The first recruiting station for the U.S. Marine Corps, known at that time as the Continental Marines, was in a bar (Tun's Tavern).

🍇 The first commercial U.S. winery, established in 1823, was located in Missouri.

🍇 Prior to the civil war, Ohio was considered America's most important wine producing state.

🍇 During prohibition, a product called the "Grape Brick" was sold to thousands of households across America. Attached to the brick of dried and pressed wine grapes was a packet of yeast, and the warning, "Do not add yeast or fermentation will result."

🍇 In 1816, the first Prohibition law went on the books in Indiana, forbidding the sale of alcohol on Sunday (still enforced to this day).

Wine & Women

1. Which of the following is an international non-profit organization designed to bring women together with wine, cheese and chocolate?
>   a.) Whole Lotta Drinking Going On
>   b.) Escapism for Women
>   c.) Wild Women on Wine
>   d.) Society for Women of Taste

2. According to *Wine for Women: A Guide to Buying, Pairing and Sharing Wine*, women account for what percentage of total wine consumers?
>   a.) 34%
>   b.) 72%
>   c.) 16%
>   d.) 64%

3. The first female winemaker in California was 31 years old when she founded her winery. Her name was:
>   a.) Josephine Tychson
>   b.) Lily Langtree
>   c.) Kate Warfield
>   d.) Isabelle Simi Haigh

4. What was the first magazine dedicated specifically to wine and women?
>   a.) Women Uncorked
>   b.) Wine Adventure Magazine
>   c.) In The Kitchen With Wine
>   d.) Women's Wine Monthly

 Solutions on page 244

WINTER PORT COMPOTE

You can bring a little summer back on one of those blustery winter days, with this easy to fix, sweet, and tart dessert and get your daily dose of vitamins, iron, and fiber too.

Difficulty: 🍷🍷
Preparation Time: 20 minutes plus chilling time
Yield: 8 servings

2 cups Ruby or Vintage Port
2 cups water
1/4 cup sugar
3 medium cinnamon sticks (3-inch size)
1/2 pound Chukar dried bing cherries
1/2 pound mixed dried fruit
Sour cream
Walnuts or almonds, slivered (optional)

1. Bring Port, water, and sugar to a boil in a stainless steel or enamel sauce pan. Add cinnamon sticks and dried fruits, (use Chukar Cherries, or if not available, you may use any dried fruits of your choice). Reduce heat and allow to simmer covered until fruit has absorbed liquid and is soft (10 to 15 minutes).

2. Remove from heat, cool to room temperature, then place in refrigerator covered until well chilled. Serve in bowls with a dollop or two of sour cream. You may sprinkle slivered toasted almonds or chopped walnuts over the top for added complexity. Serve with a small glass of Port.

Contributed by Hinzerling Winery

ZABAGLIONE

Difficulty: 🍷🍷
Preparation Time: 20 minutes
Yield: 4 servings

4 egg yolks
1/3 cup sugar
Dash of salt
1/2 cup cream Marsala wine
Fresh strawberries or raspberries
Vanilla ice cream

1. In top of a double boiler, combine egg yolks, sugar, salt and wine. Blend well. Cook over simmering water. (Water should never touch the top of the double boiler.) While cooking, beat mixture with an electric mixer until stiff peaks form, about 5 minutes.

2. Serve warm over vanilla ice cream. Garnish with berries.

1 This deep-colored French hybrid, dating from early 1960s, is commonly added to table wines to achieve the desired wine color.
   a.) Chambourcin
   b.) Counoise
   c.) Malbec
   d.) Cinsaut

2 There are four main styles of Madeira and they take their names from the grapes of which they are made. Which is not a style of Madeira?
   a.) Bual (Boal)
   b.) Malvasia(Malmsy)
   c.) Palomino
   d.) Sercial

Solutions: 1. a. Chambourcin. ; 2. c. Palomino.

Buzz on the Vine — Rudy — John and Shari Rudy — Pg.227 Pg.233

Cellar Challenge — John and Shari Rudy

Corkboard — Rudy — Pg.230

Wine Words — Rudy — Pg.221

Wine Wisdom — Rudy — Pg.224 Pg.232

Wine Wit — Rudy — Pg.235

MISCELLANEOUS

AVOCADO DRESSING

Enjoy this dressing on lettuce wedges or inside fajitas.

Difficulty: ♈
Preparation Time: 15 minutes plus chilling time
Yield: 6 servings

1 ripe avocado
1/4 cup sour cream
1 tablespoon lemon juice
3/4 teaspoon onion salt
1/4 teaspoon Worcestershire sauce
3 ounces crumbled blue cheese
1/3 cup canola oil
1/4 cup Chardonnay
1/4 cup white wine vinegar

1. Slice avocado in half and remove pit. Scoop the avocado out of the peel and mash with a fork until smooth. Stir in the sour cream, lemon juice, onion salt and Worcestershire.

2. In another bowl, mash together cheese, oil, wine and vinegar. Mix this with the avocado mixture until well blended. Cover and chill for at least 3 hours for flavors to absorb.

WINE WORDS

Part Two *"Winemaking", Continued from Page 206*

❦ *Tannins* – The compound derived from the grapes seeds, skins, stalks and stems. It accounts for the wine's astringency and help wines preserve well as they age. Tannin management is a winemakers key concern in red wine production.

❦ *Terrior* – A French term that is now used universally, terrior refers to all the elements of where a grape is grown that affects the wine's aromatic and flavor profile. These elements include: soil, rainfall, sun exposure, and a myriad of others.

❦ *Varietals* – This term refers to the actual grape that is used to produce a wine. At least 75% of the wine's grapes must be from that grape variety to bear its name, i.e. Pinot Noir, Merlot, Chardonnay, etc.

❦ *Vigneron* – A grape grower. Many in the wine industry have nothing to do with the production side of wine.

❦ *Vintage* – Year that grapes were harvested and the wine resulting from that harvest. To list the vintage on a bottle, 95% of the grapes must have been harvested in that year.

❦ *Viticulture* – The science, art and philosophy of grape production for the making of wine

❦ *Viticultural Area* – Set apart from other areas, these well-defined regions share common climate, soil, elevation and other physical features.

❦ *Yield* – The amount of wine or grapes produced in a given area. The conversion of the weight of grapes translated into wine will vary upon the pressing, grape variety, and style of wine produced.

BLOCK PARTY PUNCH

In our Kentucky days, we enjoyed this at the Fourth of July fireworks neighborhood party.

Difficulty: 🍷🍷
Preparation Time: 1 hour plus setting time
Yield: 100 servings

1 gallon green tea
Juice from 20 lemons
2 1/2 pounds brown sugar
1 gallon dry white wine
1 gallon rum
1/2 gallon Hennessy Brandy
1/2 gallon dry gin
1/2 gallon whiskey
1 quart cherries
1 quart pineapple cubes
5 quarts Champagne

1. In a large container or tub, mix the tea and lemon juice. Add brown sugar, wine, rum, brandy, gin and whiskey. Mix well. Let the mixture set for 1 1/2 to 2 weeks in a *covered* container.

2. When ready for your party, place a large block of ice into an appropriately sized container or tub. Pour the mixture over the ice block. Slowly add cherries, pineapple and Champagne and mix in a circular motion.

CARNIVAL LEMONADE

Difficulty: ♟
Preparation Time: 15 minutes plus chilling time
Yield: 6 servings

3 tablespoons sugar
Juice from 4 large lemons
1 1/2 cups cold water
1 bottle Carnival wine or Muscat or Reisling (4% residual sugar or above)

1. Place sugar and water in a pan and heat until sugar is dissolved. Cool in refrigerator for at least 30 minutes.

2. In pitcher, mix together water and sugar mixture and add lemon juice. Add desired amount of ice.

3. Add 2 parts Carnival wine to 1 part lemonade and ice. Use more or less wine as desired.

Contributed by Chef Max Duley of Peju Province Winery

CHAMPAGNE PUNCH

Difficulty: ♟
Preparation Time: 15 minutes
Yield: 20 servings

1 1/2 cups sugar
2 cups lemon juice
2 bottles Sauvignon Blanc, chilled
1 bottle Champagne, chilled
Sliced lemons, strawberries and oranges

1. Combine sugar and lemon juice. Stir until dissolved. Pour over ice in a punch bowl.

2. Add white wine and Champagne. Mix well and float fruit slices on top.

WINEWISDOM

"No poem was ever written by a drinker of water."
~Horace~

"Wine prepares the heart for love . . ."
~Ovid~

"Then a smile and a glass and a toast and a cheer, for all the good wine, and we've some of it here."
~Oliver Wendell Holmes~

". . . and we meet with Champagne and a chicken at last!"
~Lady Mary Wortley Montagu~

"When wine enlivens the heart, may friendship surround the table."
~Anonymous~

"Wine is the most healthful and hygienic of all beverages."
~Louis Pasteur~

"Although man is already 90% water, the Prohibitionists are not yet satisfied."
~John Kendrick Bangs~

"In Europe then we thought of wine as something as healthy and normal as food and also as a great giver of happiness and well being and delight."
~Ernest Hemingway~

"Drinking wine is a part of life, like eating food."
~Francis Ford Coppola~

"A glass of Sherry before dinner will revive a tired old man and whet his appetite."
~Old English Proverb~

GEORGE WASHINGTON'S EGGNOG

This is from George Washington's recipe archives. He forgot to mention how many eggs to use.

Difficulty: 🍷🍷
Preparation Time: 10 minutes plus setting time
Yield: 16 servings

1 pint brandy
1/2 pint rye whiskey
1/2 pint Jamaican rum
1/4 pint Sherry
? eggs, separated
12 tablespoons sugar
1 quart milk
1 quart cream

1. Mix brandy, whiskey, rum and Sherry.

2. Beat egg yolks in large bowl and add sugar, mixing well. Add liquor mixture to yolks drop by drop at first, slowly beating. Add milk and cream, slowly beating.

3. Beat whites of eggs until stiff and fold slowly into mixture. Let set in cool place for several days. Taste frequently.

Taste Frequently!

GRILLED PINEAPPLE SALSA

Use this dish as a dipping sauce for corn chips or as an accompaniment to grilled fish, pork or chicken.

Difficulty: 🍷🍷
Preparation Time: 20 minutes plus chilling time
Yield: 2 cups

Half of a fresh pineapple
4 scallions, thinly sliced
2 cloves garlic, minced
2 stalks lemon grass, bottom 2-inches of each peeled and minced
1 jalapeño pepper, finely chopped
1/4 cup mixture of parsley, cilantro and mint, chopped
1 teaspoon salt
1/2 cup Muscat Canelli

1. Peel the pineapple, remove any remaining eyes and core.

2. Slice into half-inch thick rings and grill over medium coals to obtain some good color, but not blackened.

3. Remove from the heat and coarsely chop.

4. Place in a bowl with remaining ingredients. Allow several hours for the flavors to meld before serving.

Contributed by Husch Vineyards

Chateau d' Yquem Sauternes (1787) is the most expensive commercially available wine. Prices range from $56,000 to $64,000 per bottle, depending on the retailer. Classified as a Premier Grand Cru, this sauterne was highly favored by Thomas Jefferson, who subsequently introduced it to George Washington.

Do you know your white wine grapes?

1. This grape is an international superstar in the wine world. It is hardy and versatile. It can take on a wide range of scents and aromas.
    a) Chablis
    b) Gewürztraminer
    c) Chenin Blanc
    d) Chardonnay

2. The term "Blanc de Noir" refers to:
    a) White wine made from grapes with thin skins
    b) White wine made from red/black grapes.
    c) White wine made from a blend or 3 or more grapes
    d) White wine made from white grapes

3. Which table, raisin and wine grape has more than 200 sub-varieties and ranges in color from pale yellow to nearly black?
    a) Muscat
    b) Sémillon
    c) Voignier
    d) Chenin Blanc

4. Germany is famous for using this grape to produce some of the finest white wines in the world. This grape, rarely blended with others, is named:
    a) Riesling
    b) Fiano
    c) Chardonnay
    d) Pinot Gris

 Solutions on page 244

ICED SHERRY COBBLER

Difficulty: ♀
Preparation Time: 5 minutes
Yield: 4 servings

1 1/2 tablespoons confectioner's sugar
1 teaspoon fresh lemon juice
3/4 cup crushed ice
1 cup Sherry

Place sugar and lemon juice in a tumbler. Add ice and then pour Sherry over all. Pour from tumbler to tumbler to mix. Serve in Sherry glasses.

*Forgive me,
for I have Zinned*

KEITH'S PEACH SORBET

Difficulty: ♀
Preparation Time: 10 minutes plus freezing time
Yield: 6 servings

8 large, fresh peaches, peeled and pitted
Juice of 1 lemon
1 cup Sauvignon Blanc
1/2 cup honey
Mint sprigs or peach slices for garnish (optional)

Purée peaches, lemon juice, wine and honey in a blender. Freeze in an ice cream maker according to directions. Serve to cleanse your pallet in between courses with garnishes if desired.

MANGO BOYSENBERRY MIMOSAS

The boysenberry garnish gives this drink a delightful color contrast.
Get creative with your juice concentrate choices for different flavor
combinations.

Difficulty: ♟
Preparation Time: 15 minutes
Yield: 10 servings

2 cups frozen, unsweetened boysenberries, thawed
2 tablespoons sugar
3 cups chilled orange juice (don't use fresh squeezed)
1 1/2 cups frozen orange-peach-mango juice concentrate
One 750 ml bottle of chilled dry Champagne
10 small orange slices

1. Place 10 berries in freezer to reserve for garnish. Purée remaining berries in a food processor. Strain through a sieve over a bowl, pressing out solids. Mix in sugar and set aside.

2. Whisk orange juice and concentrate together in a tall pitcher. Mix in Champagne. Divide mimosas among 10 Champagne glasses. Drizzle 1 1/2 teaspoons of berry purée over each. Garnish with orange slices and reserved berries.

"Here's to cold nights,
warm friends,
and a good drink to give them".
– Author unknown

CORKBOARD

When Magellan sailed around the world in 1519, more was spent on Sherry than on weapons for the voyage.

The Benedictine monk Dom Perignon (1640-1715), became cellar master at the Abbey of Hautvilliers at age 28. He invented the mushroom shaped cork and wire cage that allowed sparkling wine to be safely bottled. Previous attempts had failed as all the corks had popped. Dom lost his vision at some stage of life, which some say enhanced his senses of taste and smell.

According to Guinness World Records, the world's oldest known wooden vat or cask is still in use at the Hugel et Fils wine estate (founded 1639) in Riquewihr, Haut-Rhin, France. Twelve generations of the Hugel family have used it for winemaking since 1715.

Maribor, Slovenia boasts the oldest known grapevine in the world. Approximately 400 years old, it is carefully pruned each year with a cutting presented to selected communities around the world as a gesture of goodwill and friendship. The vine is featured on an illustration dating back to 1681. It yields enough grapes

As late as the mid-17th century, the French wine makers did not use corks. Instead, they used oil-soaked rags stuffed into the necks of bottles.

The Irish believe that fairies are extremely fond of good wine. According to Irish folklore, royalty would leave a barrel of wine out for the fairies at night. Sure enough, it would always be gone in the morning.

Portuguese wine bottled in 1811 is called "comet wine". Its excellent quality was believed to be due to the Great Comet of that year. The term "comet wine" is often used for any wine made in the year of an important comet, and has recently been used to describe a wine of superior quality.

"The old gentleman yet nurses some few bottles of the famous comet year (i.e. 1811), emphatically called comet wine." –*The Times.*

MARINADE FOR BEEF

Warm this marinade and serve over grilled meat, or use it cold as a sauce for picnic sandwiches of grilled beef served open-faced on pumpernickel.

Difficulty: ⏛
Preparation Time: 15 minutes plus standing time
Yield: Enough for 5 pounds of beef

1/2 cup cooking oil
1/4 cup red wine vinegar
1/2 cup tomato purée
1/2 cup prepared marinara sauce
1/4 cup Burgundy wine
1/2 cup dry Sherry
1/2 teaspoon salt
1/4 teaspoon onion salt
1/4 teaspoon garlic salt
1/4 teaspoon pepper

Mix all ingredients in a large casserole. Place sliced, cooled beef (not too thick) in the marinade. Refrigerate, covered, overnight or at least 12 hours.

WineWisdom

"Wine is a constant proof that God loves us and loves to see us happy."
~Benjamin Franklin~

"Wine is one of the most civilized things in the world and . . . it offers a greater range for enjoyment and appreciation than possibly any other purely sensory thing which may be purchased."
~Ernest Hemingway~

"A warm toast. Good company. A fine wine. May you enjoy all three."
~Anonymous~

"Where there is no wine, there is no love."
~Euripides~

"Bacchus opens the gate of the heart."
~Latin Proverb~

"Wine is the divine juice of September."
~Francois Voltaire~

"When a man drinks wine at dinner he begins to be better pleased with himself."
~Plato~

"Drink no longer water but use a little wine for thy stomach's sake."
~I Timothy 5:23~

"Wine, wit and wisdom. Wine enough to sharpen wit, Wit enough to give zest to wine, Wisdom enough to stop at the right time."
~Anonymous~

"The best kind of wine is that which is most pleasant to him who drinks it."
~Pliny~

CELLAR CHALLENGE

Home Sweet Home

Champagne is French. Shiraz is Australian. Can you match the style of wine with the country below?

a. France   b. Germany   c. Italy   d. Spain   e. Other

1. Chianti
2. Macabeo
3. Airén
4. Burgundy
5. Valpolicella
6. Chablis
7. Silvaner
8. Cava
9. Lambrusco
10. Retsina
11. Soave
12. Vin Spumos

13. Sekt
14. Orvieto
15. Meursault
16. Gumza
17. Frascati
18. Trollinger
19. Moscatel
20. Rioja
21. Txacolí
22. Barolo
23. Bordeaux
24. Pamid

 Solutions on page 244

"Sorrow can be alleviated by good sleep, a bath and a glass of wine."
~St. Thomas Aquinas

"The smell of wine, oh how much more delicate, cheerful, gratifying, celestial and delicious it is than that of oil."
~Rabelias in Gargantua (1534)

MUSCAT CREAM FOR PUMPKIN PIE
Difficulty: ♥♥
Preparation Time: 15 minutes plus cooling time
Yield: 6 Servings

1/4 cup plus 2 tablespoons Orange Muscat
2 tablespoons sugar
1 cup heavy cream
1 pumpkin pie
Whole nutmeg (optional)

1. Place 1/4 cup Muscat in non-reactive sauce pan. Add sugar; simmer until reduced to a thick syrup. Transfer to small cup; set aside to cool.

2. Whip cream until soft peaks form.

3. Add 2 tablespoons wine to dissolve in syrup. Whip syrup mixture into cream and spread on top of pie. Scrape a little nutmeg on top and enjoy. Covers one 8-inch pie.

Contributed by Stevenot Winery

PINOT GRIS MINT TEA
Difficulty: ♥
Preparation time: 10 minutes
Yield: 6 servings

10 fresh mint leaves
2 cups water
3 unflavored tea bags
1/2 bottle Pinot Gris
2 cups lemonade
1/4 cup sugar (adjust to taste)

1. Bring water to boil in a 4-quart saucepan. Add tea bags and mint. Reduce heat and let simmer for 5 minutes.

2. Remove from heat. Remove tea bags and add Pinot Gris, lemonade and sugar. Stir well and serve over ice with additional mint leaves.

wine wit

Does a bear spit in the woods?

SANGRIA

Difficulty: ▼
Preparation time: 15 minutes
Yield: 12 servings

1 liter dry red wine
2 ounces Cointreau or other orange liqueur
2 ounces brandy
4 tablespoons sugar
Champagne or club soda
1 lemon, seeded and sliced
1 orange, seeded and sliced
1 apple, seeded and sliced

Mix the first 4 ingredients in a 2-liter container or decanter. Add Champagne or club soda to fill the remainder of container just before serving. Serve in well-chilled wine glasses garnished with fruit slices or over cracked ice in a punch bowl with the fruit floating on top.

SPOOM

Serve spoom to cleanse the palate between courses or as a refreshing dessert.

Difficulty: 🍷🍷
Preparation Time: 15 minutes plus freezing time
Yield: 12 servings

1 cup granulated sugar
1/2 cup water
4 egg whites
2 pints lemon sherbet, softened
2 cups Champagne

1. Bring sugar and water to a boil in a medium saucepan, stirring until sugar dissolves. Continue cooking, without stirring, until mixture reaches 238°F on a candy thermometer.

2. Meanwhile, beat egg whites in a large mixing bowl until soft peaks form. Beating constantly, slowly pour hot sugar syrup over egg whites until blended. Stir in sherbet.

3. Spoon mixture into 12 dessert glasses. Cover and freeze until firm. Sprinkle with Champagne before serving.

"I love waking up in the morning not knowing what I'm going to do or who I'm going to meet. Just yesterday I was sleeping under a bridge, and today I'm on the grandest liner in the world drinking champagne with you fine people. I'll have some more please."
~Jack Dawson in *Titanic* (1997)

"Champagne yes, philosophy no."
~Kit Moresby in *The Sheltering Sky* (1990)

"I'm only a beer teetotaler, not a champagne teetotaler. I don't like beer."
~George Bernard Shaw, *Candida* (1898)

WINE MUSTARD SAUCE

This sauce is delicious on sandwiches and with sausages. If you can't find wine mustard online or at your local wine shop or winery, try this as an alternative.

Difficulty: ♟
Preparation Time: 15 minutes
Yield: 2 cups

1 1/2 cups mustard
1/2 cup dry white wine
2 tablespoons sugar
1 teaspoon salt
2 tablespoons flour
1/4 cup water

1. Combine mustard, wine, sugar and salt in a saucepan. Bring to a boil, stirring constantly.

2. In a bowl, combine flour and water. Stir into the mustard mixture. Reduce heat and simmer for 10 minutes until thickened, stirring constantly.

*"May the best day of your past,
be the worst day of your future."*
– Unknown

PHYSICAL ACTIVITY

The United States Department of Agriculture (USDA) recommends physical activity as part of the new Food Guide Pyramid. We have some suggestions:

Juice fruits without the assistance of any gadgets. Squeeze, release, squeeze, release . . .

Strategically place ingredients on opposite countertops. Use lunges to retrieve them.

Pick any style you like, corkscrews or Champagne cages. Both offer a chance for some upper body conditioning: Twisting, turning, pumping and pulling. Now the real trick is getting the cork back into the bottle.

Even after your wine dish is in the oven, repeat your "oven-door hip closing" move 20 times on the right. Rotate and repeat on the left.

Take brisk walks to and from the market to purchase more wine.

Celebrate each finished wine masterpiece you prepare by developing your own special kitchen dance. Once polished, you may want to perform this dance while serving your dish to guests.

While grating and zesting, exhale on the down stroke and inhale on the upstroke.

Whisk ingredients briskly. Rotate direction every 20 times around the bowl. Switch arms and repeat.

Follow Lucy & Ethel's example and try a round of aerobic grape stomping. Fill a half barrel with grapes, take off your shoes and stomp vigorously until you've juiced them all. Strain (the grapes, not you) and enjoy the juice. We've done this, and trust us, it's not easy!

SOLUTIONS

CRAINS CHALLENGES
Page 8 , Movie Quotes:

1. (d) Mary and George offer a brief speech at the Martinis' in *It's a Wonderful Life* (1946)
2. (b) Two-Face in *Batman Forever* (1995).
3. (i) Dr. Hannibal Lecter in *Silence of the Lambs* (1991)
4. (e) Steve Martin as Navin in *The Jerk* (1979)
5. (g) Porthos in *The Three Musketeers* (1993)
6. (j) Dracula in Dracula: *Dead and Loving It* (1995)
7. (a) Miles to Jack, as he smells a wine they are sampling in *Sideways* (2004)
8. (c) James Bond in *Goldfinger* (1964)
9. (h) Waiter Steve Martin, in *The Muppet Movie* (1979)
10. (f) W. C. Fields in *Never Give a Sucker an Even Break* (1941)

VEGETABLES CHALLENGES
Page 31, Do You Know Your Bubbly?:

1. (b) In 1974, Moët et Chandon became the first French Champagne house to open shop in California.
2. (c) Cava is translated to mean "cellar", referring to large underground cellars for aging wine.
3. (b) Germany produces a considerable number of sparkling wines that are made using the charmat method.
4. (d) 49 million bubbles are in each bottle.

FRUITS CHALLENGES
Page 76 , Do You Know Your Red Wine Grapes?:

1. (d) The Shiraz/Syrah grape produces powerful black, aromatic wines that age magnificently.
2. (c) Tests at U.C. Davis in California showed that Cabernet Sauvignon is the result of a blend of Cabernet Franc and Sauvignon Blanc.
3. (b) This versatile grape can produce heavy to medium-weight reds, rosés and blush wines. The White Zinfandel craze of the 1970s created tremendous interest in this grape.
4. (c) Yes, Miles was referring to Merlot. Merlot-based wines usually have medium body and may be described as displaying hints of berry, blackberry, plum, tobacco or licorice.

Page 83, Did You Know?:

1. (a) Estimates suggest that Trebianno/Ugni Blanc produces more wine than any other variety in the world.
2. (d) German immigrants planted vines on the banks of the Missouri River, in an area that became known as the Rhineland of Missouri.
3. (b) Botrytis cinerea, or noble rot, is a fungus that is desirable under certain circumstances.
4. (b) Refosco is believed to have been the favorite wine of Caesar's second wife, Livia.

MILK CHALLENGES
Page 97, Wine in the Grand Ole United States:

1. (a) California is the market leader, followed by Washington, New York, Oregon and Texas.
2. (b) Brotherhood Winery is located in New York's Hudson Valley.
3. (d) David Lett of Eyrie Vineyard planted the first Pinot Noir vines in Oregon in 1965.
4. (b) Yakima Valley, which currently boasts more than 40 wineries, was the first AVA in Washington.

Page 116, Host a Wine and Cheese Party:

Set 1:

  1. (e) Tawny Port – Blue Cheese/Roquefort

  2. (d) Sparkling Wine – Brie

  3. (f) White Zinfandel – Cream Cheese

  4. (a) Beaujolais – Feta

  5. (c) Riesling – Monterey Jack

  6. (b) Chardonnay – Provolone

Set 2:

  1. (b) Chardonnay – Goat Cheese

  2. (d) Sparkling Wine – Gouda

  3. (f) Who Eats Limburger? – Limburger

  4. (d) Light Red or White – Mozzarella

  5. (a) Cabernet Sauvignon – Sharp Cheddar

  6. (c) Gewürztraminer, Riesling – Swiss

A sharp cheddar or blue cheese doesn't go well with a delicate Riesling. A harder cheese goes best with a more tannic red. It takes some time to understand pairings, and the key is to discover what tastes best to you. Perhaps the best summary on pairing wine and cheese comes from wine expert Josh Wesson, "Don't have the wine step all over the food nor the food step all over the wine. Two different flavors can be synergistic, producing a third flavor experience."

MEATS CHALLENGES

Page 123, Do You Know Your World Wine Regions?:

  1. True.

  2 True.

  3. False. The Venice region is Italy's leader in the production of classified
wine; primarily Soave, Bardolino and Valpolicella.

  4. False. The south-western Spanish province of Andalucía offers more vineyard acreage than anywhere else in the world.

  5. True.

  6. False. Chardonnay is the most widely planted grape in New Zealand.

  7. True.   8. True.

  9. True.   10. True.

Page 149, Color Me . . . If You Can:

White or Red:

1. Red	16. Red
2. White	17. White
3. Red	18. Red
4. Red	19. White
5. White	20. White
6. Red	21. Red
7. White	22. White
8. White	23. White
9. White	24. Red
10. Red	25. Red
11. Red	26. White
12. Red	27. Red
13. White	28. Red
14. Red	29. White
15. Red	30. Red

Word Scramble Solutions:

1. Merlot	6. Chenin Blanc
2. Cabernet	7. Riesling
3. Pinot Noir	8. Semillon
4. Sangiovese	9. Chardonnay
5. Syrah	10. Muscat

DESSERTS CHALLENGES

Page 203, Dessert Wine: Here's to Your Sweet Tooth:

1. (d) Canada is the largest producer of ice wines, utilizing a variety of grapes that include Rieslings.

2. (b) Australian dessert wines are nicknamed "stickies". This is a reference to the wonderful "sticky" texture of these wines as they flow across the palate.

3. (a) Genuine Sherry is made from white grapes in the southernmost part of Spain.

4. (c) Wood Ports spend all their lives maturing in casks. Examples include: Ruby, Tawny and White Port.

Page 216, Wine and Women:

1. (c) Wild Women on Wine was inspired by an annual trip of 6 girlfriends. Their stated goal is to encourage women to take time to relax and enjoy life.
2. (d) Consumption of wine in the U.S. has risen steadily over the past decade. Trends such as an increased interest in gourmet cooking and dining have been behind this increase. And yes, women account for nearly 64% of all wine consumers.
3. (a) Josephine made wine at Tychson Hill Vineyard for eight years, beginning in 1886. Popular varietals she produced at the time were Zinfandel, Reisling and Burgundy.
4. (b) Wine Adventure Magazine was launched by Michele Ostrove in July, 2005. This magazine merges food, travel, and culture through the universal connection of wine.

MISCELLANEOUS CHALLENGES
Page 227, Do You Know Your White Wine Grapes?:

1. (d) Chardonnay has a more neutral taste, which causes some to call it boring and chant: "ABC, "Anything But Chardonnay."
2. (b) White wine, especially sparkling wine, made from red/black grapes is referred to as "Blanc de Noir".
3. (a) Muscat is also credited as being the oldest known variety of grape.
4. (a) Riesling is one of the few white wines which ages well. Its color is normally clear and becomes golden with age.

Page 233, Home Sweet Home:

1. c.) Italy
2. d.) Spain
3. d.) Spain
4. a.) France
5. c.) Italy
6. a.) France
7. b.) Germany
8. d.) Spain
9. c.) Italy
10. e.) Greece
11. c.) Italy
12. e.) Romania
13. b.) Germany
14. c.) Italy
15. d.) France
16. e.) Bulgaria
17. c.) Italy
18. b.) German
19. e.) Portugal
20. d.) Spain
21. d.) Spain
22. c.) Italy
23. a.) France
24. e.) Bulgaria

Asked when she drinks champagne, Madam Lilly Bollinger replied, "I drink it when I'm happy and when I'm sad. Sometimes I drink it when I'm alone. When I have company, I consider it obligatory. I trifle with it if I'm not hungry and drink it when I am. Otherwise, I never touch it----unless I'm thirsty."